D1176238

B Colette   c.1
Colette
  The blue lantern

BIOGRAPHY   C.1

COLETTE, SIDONIE
GABRIELLE

THE BLUE LANTERN

DISCARDED

all losses shall be made good to the satisfaction of the
Librarian.
    4. Each borrower is held responsible for all books
drawn on his card and for all fines accruing on the same.

bd
INDUSTRIES   PRINTED IN U.S.A.

The Blue Lantern

Sidonie Gabrielle **COLETTE**

The Blue Lantern

Translated by Roger Senhouse

NEW YORK / *Farrar, Straus and Company*

YUMA COUNTY
LIBRARY DISTRICT
350 3rd Ave. Yuma, AZ 85364
(928) 782-1871
www.yumalibrary.org

English translation of *Le Fanal Bleu* from
the *Fleuron* edition *Oeuvres completes de Colette
de l'Academie Goncourt*, Vol. XIV, 1950.
Copyright © 1963 by Martin Secker & Warburg Limited
Library of Congress catalog card number 63-19563
Manufactured in the United States of America
First printing, 1963

B
Colette
c.1

McClurg
3.95
11-14-'63

I

W E should not be unreasonably perturbed when our precious senses become dulled with age. I say " we ", but I am the text of my own sermon. My chief concern is lest I should mistake the true nature of a condition which has come upon me gradually. It can be given a name: it keeps me in a state of vigilance, of uncertainty, ready to accept whatever may fall to my lot. The prospect gives rise to little that is reassuring, but I have no choice.

More than once of late, turning my eyes from my book or my blue-tinted writing paper towards the superb quadrangle that I am privileged to view from my window, I have thought 'The children in the Garden are not nearly so noisy this year,' and a moment later found myself finding fault with the door bell, the telephone, and the whole orchestral gamut of the radio for becoming progressively fainter. As for the china lamp—not the blue lantern that burns by day and night, of course, but the pretty one with flowers and arabesques painted on it—I was for ever scolding it unjustly: 'What can this wretched thing have been eating to make it so heavy?' Discoveries, ever more discoveries! Things always explain themselves in the long run. Instead, then, of landing on new islands of discovery, is my course set for the open sea where there is no sound other than that of the lonely

5

DISCARDED

heart-beat comparable to the pounding of the surf? Rest assured, nothing is decaying, it is I who am drifting. . . . The open sea, but not the wilderness. The discovery that there is no wilderness! That in itself is enough to sustain me in triumphing over my afflictions.

Four years have gone by since *L'Etoile Vesper* was published; years that sped speedily enough as they must when the mornings are all alike and the evenings are spent in a kind of glass retort, with some unpredictable little incident at the centre, like a kernel. I was honest when I called *L'Etoile Vesper* my last book. I have come to see that it is as difficult to stop writing as it is uncomfortable to go on. Beneath my blue lantern, my life-line grows ever shorter and shorter, my physical torment ever more persistent. Yet how many changes of scene—other than on foot—are still permitted me! Uriage in '46, Geneva and the Beaujolais in '47, Provence, albeit against doctor's orders, in '48. From my seat in a car or a wheel-chair, I proudly compiled a census of the landscapes, streams and shores I have rediscovered. 'After all, I can still visit these.' Visit! Yes, in a manner of speaking and, above all, of experience. During the final infirmity of her life, Anna de Noailles saw more cities, hills and oceans than I, against the backcloth of her perpetually lowered blinds.

I wanted this book to be a journal; but I do not possess the knack of writing a proper journal, that is to say of stringing together, bead by bead, day after day, a rosary whose value and intrinsic lustre are relative to the writer's powers of exact observation, of assessing his own importance and that of his time. The art of selection, of noting things of mark, retaining the unusual while discarding the commonplace, has never been mine, since most of the time I am stimulated and quickened by the ordinary. There I was, vowing never to write anything again after *L'Etoile Vesper*, and now I have covered two hundred pages which are neither memoirs nor journal. Let my reader resign himself to it: this lantern of mine, burning blue day and night between the pair of red curtains, pressed close to the window like one of the butterflies that fall asleep there on a summer morning, throws no light on events significant enough to astonish him.

It is twenty years, or a little more, since Princesse Edmond de Polignac, staunch friend of music and musicians, passed sentence with a glance and a single word on the little four-legged table-desk that used to follow me from Paris to Saint-Tropez and back, taking up its position on the bed at my night's lodging. I set great store by this piece of furniture, originally contrived for me by Luc-Albert Moreau—painter, engraver, and master carpenter —so that I could write other than in a sitting posture, my feet dangling, which has always had an adverse effect on my comfort and my work.

"I have," Princesse de Polignac said to me, "a little English piece which, if enlarged, would be just right for you."

She was not mistaken. Widened, made higher, reinforced, and stripped of most of its English eighteenth-century elegance, it bestrides my divan-bed and indeed, for a quarter of a century, has gladdened both my leisure and my working hours. An adjustable desk has been let into the solid mahogany table and takes the weight of the things I turn to for relaxation from my own writing: telephone, fruit, portable radio, and bulky illustrated volumes. This contraption glides easily from the head of the bed to my feet. Including the all-purpose knife with its scorpion handle, the bunch of fountain-pens and various knick-knacks of no particular use, I have assembled on its back a fair number of good and willing servants.

All round me a litter of papers; but a litter belied by its appearance, with more often than not, to add to the confusion, a boiled chestnut, a half-eaten apple, and for the last month a seed-pod—from some exotic plant, no doubt —the capsules of which retain for a while and then expel, almost with violence, a delicate silvery follicle weighted with a tiny seed and lighter even than thistledown. One by one these feathery tufts break loose, drift up to the warm air beneath my ceiling, float there for some time before descending, and should one of them happen to be caught by the draught from the fire it yields at once, a consenting victim, and flings itself deliberately into the flames, there to perish of its own volition. I do not know the name of the plant which scatters its winged spirits abroad in this fashion, but it has no need of a label to take its place in my dunce's museum.

What has become of those whom I wanted to last for ever, firmly attached to their own lives and mine? How could I ever have conceived that Marguerite Moreno would abandon me? She was kindly treated even by fatigue, and she would laugh me to scorn in my praise of idleness and the forty winks of a siesta. . . . But Marguerite goes and catches cold, and succumbs within a week. But Luc-Albert Moreau, happening to meet a friend, exclaims cheerfully "Hullo, old chap, how pleased I am to see you!" and dies on the spot from heart failure. And before them Léon-Paul Fargue who, on his death bed, grumbled about the blue of his sheets which he had had dyed: "Far too blue . . . won't do at all." And others there are too whom I must give up trying to name, or even count. In my heart of hearts I blame them for dying, calling them careless, imprudent. How could they deprive me of their company, and so abruptly, how could they think of doing such a thing to me! So I have banished from sight and mind the vision of them lying prone and lifeless for ever. Fargue turned suddenly to stone? I'll have none of it. My Fargue is still wearing his dusty walking-shoes, still talking, scratching the head of his black cat, is still ringing me up, still tramping from Lipp to Ménilmontant, and berating his bed for its too maritime blue. . . . Marguerite Moreno's feet still shod with static gold? Certainly not! They live in my memory as they were, wayward, restless, vulnerable and never tired.

My juniors in the prime of life sometimes look sternly at me; they feel anxious. They gather the recalcitrant fold of a shawl across my shoulder with a "You're not feeling a draught?". No, I am not feeling chilly, I am not feeling *that particular* draught you have in mind. My thoughts are too out of joint for me to feel it. I have so many reasons for avoiding what you tactfully call "the dangerous draught". Chief among them is pain, pain ever young and active, instigator of astonishment, of

anger, imposing its rhythm on me, provoking me
to defy it; the pain that enjoys an occasional respite
but does not want my life to end: happily I have pain.
Oh, I know perfectly well that by using the adverb
"happily" I sound affected, like someone putting on the
brave smile of an invalid! Very few invalids do remain
entirely natural, but I would not like it thought that I
am making my infirmity an occasion for sinful pride, that
I require respect and special consideration, or that it
fosters an inferiority complex, that root cause of acerbity.
I am not referring to those who pretend to be sufferers,
who are of no interest and are in any case a small
minority, nor am I alluding to a category of sufferers who
are far from reluctant when surprised or discovered in
the very act of suffering. My doctor-brother summed up
in a few words the pleasure enjoyed by such as these.
"It is," he said, "a kind of ecstasy. It's akin to scratching
the hollow of your ear with a match-stalk. Aphrodisiacal,
almost."

A prominent politician, who was lame, once confided
something to me which I had no difficulty in understanding, though at the time I was myself in excellent health.
This man of politics liked to elevate my mind to the
realm of general ideas, at least he made a good try. I
struggled to follow his line of thought, but not for very
long. I believe he would have found me mediocre all in
all had he not so enjoyed one of my books, *Break of Day*,
and had he not wished to expand (I would have said
'restrict') the scope of my life by the help of some great
idea that should serve me as, in a sense, religion, high
purpose (his phrase), inspiration. Out of malice and to
get my own back, I asked him one day whether he could

conceive of what a life laid waste by a single idea would
be like, and I was astonished by his unhesitating reply:
"Perfectly well, since all my life long, every day and
almost at every hour, I have remembered that I was
lame."

Up to the time of his untimely death he endured with
great fortitude one accident and operation after another,
and his legacy to us was a considerable corpus of learned
works entirely devoted, as had been his life, to political
matters—all, that is, save one, a story of some length, in
its way a masterpiece, a single story whose hero was a
cripple.

So, as luck will have it, I am fated to suffer pain, which
I reconcile with a gambler's spirit, my ultra-feminine
gambler's spirit, my instinct for the game of life, if you
prefer it; the Last Cat, towards the end of her life, gave
every indication by the movement of a paw, by the smile
on her face, that a trailing piece of string was still for her
a plaything, food for feline thought and illusion. Those
who surround me will never let me want for pieces of
string.

✍ II *Geneva 1946*

I AM just back from Geneva, where life is brisk and not too noisy. To start with I found little resemblance between the peculiar existence of an invalid-under-treatment in the heart of a foreign town and my customary way of life, adapted over the years and so ungrudgingly to the dictates of a disease with its contrasting ups and downs, and to a beloved city where I hardly had need of pain to equip me for an imitation of the thebaic life in Egypt, with its discretionary solitude and chance sociability.

Confined to my downstairs quarters, I neither heard nor was affected by the teeming life of the Swiss capital. True enough, its roadways are well laid and its traffic largely consists of noiseless vehicles. Early in the morning a hand-cart collects the leaves and twigs from the little square. And the waste paper? Certainly not! In Geneva no litter is left lying about. The little hand-cart rolls along on two large pneumatic tyres. My window looked out on a length of embankment, a street corner, and all I could see from it were sleek automobiles gleaming like brand new pianos.

The first weeks of a prolonged treatment brought me both renewed pain and respite from it, if prostration can be regarded as a lull. I only had to recall my

brief periodic visits to Geneva thirty years earlier, in a
family pension where theatrical and music-hall artistes,
whose purses were as modestly lined as my own,
frequented a table d'hôte. A Geneva under pouring rain.
My pockets were stuffed with cigarettes for the needs of
others (I don't smoke), and tiny gun-metal or nickel
watches costing ten francs apiece, in the days when the
Swiss franc and the French were equivalent.

Back in Geneva in 1946, while timid April reluctantly
approached, I looked forward to the return of some of my
strength, or rather of some of my optimism—the two are
really one and the same—if not the decisive killing of my
pain; and also to the time when an almost exclusively
physical dread would so far yield as to grant me a keener
perception of the town and its inmates. Had I, then, been
reduced to such straits that, to start with, the mountain of
solid silver on the far side of Lac Léman appeared to me
as no different from its picture postcard replicas? Believe
this I must, for I regarded the towering plume of water
which, spurting from the lake, remains erect and bran-
dished aloft before constantly returning to it, as little
more than a glorified toy, a blade of corn, or seed-corn at
the mercy of the wind yet ever resistant. Believe it I must,
for at first I could not bring myself to curb a sense of
dependence and humility in front of the therapeutist who
had undertaken to act in my defence.

In the first place I learnt how a patient should behave
under treatment: for this my doctor friends had not prepared me. I learnt how to accustom myself to punctuality
and the daily round, to the hours of visitation from an
all-powerful, well-intentioned, inexorable stranger. . . .
The hour of fearing a certain man, a man unknown,

although he was answering my summons. It happened to
be the hour that was highly charged with a persistent
coquetry, that called for a rose-pink petticoat, a new
ribbon in the night-dress, a freshly ironed dressing-gown.
The moment that precedes the entry of such a man with
healing powers quickens the pulse more than his maltreat-
ment of the limbs—injections, massage, pommellings,
vicarious deep-ray therapy, to which his visible presence
acts as alleviation. After the cry of agony wrung from
me or the muttered oath, I indulged in a wry laugh
seemlier than a sob, a hearty swear-word, or an indecent
joke for which the doctor made allowance. After that
I would enjoy a most agreeable conversation for a minute
or so, friendly, light-hearted, when I forgot all about
myself, and . . . " Good-bye till tomorrow, my dear
doctor ".

I had indeed forgotten my Geneva of other days, since
on my first carriage outings as the April dusk was falling,
I was utterly astonished to find that the town had un-
leashed a rush of pedestrians, cyclists, and noiseless
American cars: surprised at the concourse without
hubbub, activity without collision, haste without confusion. And—greatest surprise of all to me after six years
of confinement in the blue of a Paris cellar, with the
black-out of war and the red glow of a shaded torch—the
bright carnival of electricity! Bathed in a wealth of rosy
light, the small dwellings were transformed into a quivering, teeming thoroughfare, brimming over but well
ordered, where the shop windows displayed a congeries
of goods—lace, footwear, scents and food. I never ceased

to register surprise. What! Chocolate for the asking, and gâteaux, in pâtisseries still abundantly overflowing when all had eaten their fill! Also, for the asking, to quench my lips that are parched for it, can that be milk, MILK, pure and held in reverence, sold at every door! Milk that in Paris, following the war restrictions even for the old, is bluish and rationed drop by drop. Is it really true that all and sundry, myself included, can sit down here in a garden-restaurant or ice-cream parlour, and ask for a cup, nay, two and three cups of milk and be supplied! Permissible for anyone to drink it out of a red cup blobbed with white, or one blue as a periwinkle! Drink it, invisible yet palatable, from a large galactite goblet as milk-white as itself! Or ask for it at any hour in my hotel room, either iced and tasteless or warm and evocative of glossy udders, stain it with coffee, lace it, foaming and heated, with vanilla, with sugar and rum! It will be some time before I tire of seeing milk in shining canisters being carried by children all over the town, of surveying it as so many landmarks on my wheeled outings, left unprotected at the half-open wicket of a chalet, or balanced among the unripe cherries on the lower branch of a tree, or sitting in state on the little boundary wall under the watchful eye of a cat!

For anyone not able to dawdle along a pavement and indulge the fortuitous whims and luck of the stroller, there remain only superficial sights, cities that dwindle from view, buildings enhanced by alluring optical illusions. Not only am I determined, from now and henceforward to remain satisfied with this state of affairs, but I am stimulated by the prospect. What have I to lose? Nothing now. The very contrary. Illusions crowd thick upon me. What I take to be a hedging implement, can it really be the latest invention for making coffee! And surely that pretty object so elegantly curved that it looks the ideal prop for a climbing polygonum cannot possibly turn into a trouser-press! In this country a practical invention works wonders. For how long, I wonder, will certain shops, that modestly style themselves 'ironmongers', be inaccessible to me? I would dearly love at least to press my nose against their windows, become intoxicated with varnished woodwork, red beechwood, enamelled iron and aluminium, so effectively does Swiss ingenuity, at the mere sight of it, stir and quicken the idea of art and harmony. On the other hand, the less said about the arty shops full of assorted trinkets the better. . . .

But no one has suggested that I turn art critic, and enumerate landscapes, pink-fleshed nudes, still lifes; and goodness knows what use I could have for an embossed leather writing-pad or a slab of ornamental crystal! Let us give art a miss; I get as much from passing slowly in my chair in front of shops where everything on display has a new-laid look. Art, in this country means a state of innocence, the jealous care for reputation, the honest saleswoman; art and display here take the form of paper—crinkled, serrated, pleated, gilded—paper in abundance, white as snow, blue as a glacier. Compared with it and its healthy profusion, the linen of our poor France in her time of penury, eked out to the extent of using one corner of a towel after another, will be found slightly abhorrent.

Bananas, late-season but still juicy apples, early strawberries, oranges, eggs, cream whipped or plain! Against that, no cheese—other than by the gramme—no rice, no butter, except by trickery or arrangement. "What, no gruyère in Switzerland? You can't mean it!" We simply burst out laughing. We took it for a joke at our expense as newcomers, until the staid solemnity of the local inhabitants changed the look on our faces: "No, we have none for the moment," said the charming young lady, a native of Geneva. She wore well cut clothes and jewellery; but she could not procure either butter or cheese. Brought up to respect restrictions, it never entered her head to get round them. Perhaps the devil does not exist in Switzerland!

And gorged with other good things we would console ourselves with bread alone, *pain-gâteau, pain-brioche, pain-gourmandise.* So good was it that we feared giving full rein to our appetite and dared not, at table, ask for a second helping more than twice.

I have advanced only by small relays, if I dare so to express myself, in getting to know what amenities Geneva has to offer. Spring was hesitant, and from a bed of suffering one does not take any but a restricted view of the lives of the hale and hearty. My strength was at a low ebb by eight in the evening, when the tray would arrive set with raw salads, grilled meat, green vegetables and fruit —don't we all know by heart the list of a prescribed menu!—and after that came my illuminated entertainment. Through the open window, framing a blue that subtly deepens with the shades of night, I can see a stretch of the lake which reflects a bridge and quaysides, and till past midnight its confines are delineated by multicoloured electric lamps, street lamps, and strings of fairy lights. Tomorrow the early morning haze will restore to my view the iridescent cathedral, seeming almost to quiver as it is hoisted above the rooftops with its strange glazed domes that brood over its inner sanctuaries. Tomorrow I shall have the peace of a misty sunrise and the curvetting swallows. In the evening, the banners of multicoloured light dip in the lake and ripple over the surface. One particular "advertisement blue" glorifies the national clock-and-watch trade and where this azure strikes across an absinthe-green its colour is enhanced, while a deep crimson spreads out as far as the prow-like breasts of three swans poised above their own reflection.

Certainly it is a pleasure to lie facing a spectacle of lights and shades without so much as having to raise oneself on an elbow, without craning one's neck or sitting up in bed, and never to take one's eyes off it till the curtain of their lids is lowered. Whatever is easily come by is always a pleasure, even when distilled by a drop of bitterness: if I did not suffer—here and here, and again here—this . . . well, this agony, I should never have thought of positioning my bed, calculated to a nicety, in the corner where its occupant is afforded an untrammelled view of three horizons. Those who are fit and agile have no need of such convenience.

"I shall go off by myself on a shopping expedition," said a woman friend who was staying a few days in Geneva, "to buy you whatever you think might tempt you here. Let me have a list."

No sooner said than done. For a long time I had wanted

a pepper-mill, properly made, a mill, as they say in my quarter of Paris, "that grinds", and not one of those tuppeny-ha'penny little tooth-wheel objects that wear out in next to no time and can be found in any of our multiple stores at home. I also wanted a braid of thread and a braid of silk made up in the old-fashioned way in needlefuls of equal length and various colours, tied tight at either end like saveloys. I now possess them. A little too skimpy, but a pretty piece of hand-plaiting, of real *passementerie*. I wanted, too, some four-holed mother-of-pearl buttons for my underclothes. Mother-of-pearl, and I refused to go back on my word. Yes, mother-of-pearl, and may the walls come tumbling down about me! And needles, into the bargain, some "English" needles (when I was a child their glazed envelopes were already printed in German), needles which we, the mistress-craftswomen in hand-sewing, called "taper-eyed". And some darning wool, wound on cards. And elastic, to run up the waistbands for stockinette knickers. And some old-fashioned reels of cotton, waxed, for stitching leather. Have I ever stitched, do I stitch, shall I stitch leather? That's beside the point. And a twist of real silk for repairing the frayed button-holes on men's clothes. . . . Is there, then, some strange happiness to be derived from the sight and touch of certain "requisites" which have never been drastically changed or modified by any aesthetic concern or shift of fashion? There is. But since I am still fairly well-off, I do not put them to their proper use. Entranced by the magic of contemplative evocation, I deck myself out in the fine feathers of haberdashery. All the same you would never have imagined that this right hand of mine, now rather bunched up from the habit of writing, was once

endowed with the cunning to beget that show-piece of
symmetry, sober relievo, solidity: the buttonhole on a
male garment! I mean, of course, the buttonhole-stitched
buttonhole. There is no poetry in the other, the so-called
piped buttonhole.

Hunting for needles for crewel-work is labour in vain.
France is a void, Switzerland a barren desert. For ages
past the answer given me in the big shops all over France
has been: "We don't stock such things. Of course, I'm
not saying that in the past . . ." with the head on one
side, you know, rather like a dog when offered an empty
bowl, and as a consolation prize I am offered darning-
needles! I plan, when my dearest friend takes to driving
me out again and has recovered his patience, to stop at
all the little village haberdashers, the proper kind, with
a glass panelled door and tinkling bell, where buttons
are to be found in the wool basket, wool in the boot-
lace drawer, bootlaces in the zip-fastener container, where
a strong smell of pickled herring is all pervasive, and
where, finally, a small girl turns toward the murky back
of the shop with a plaintive "Mum, I can't find any-
where the sort of needles the lady is asking for!"

Six weeks. Ought I to exclaim "Already!" or "Only
six!"? The days pass, all alike, intent on running their
course, each scarred at the beginning, middle, and end
by physical pain, that sharp recall to life. Dear-Doctor-till-
tomorrow still has his gentle voice and his big heart that
takes up too much room in his big breast and makes him
wheezy. The weather is fine—no, it's going to be fine.
Covered by cloud, a white sun is melting the snows on

the flanks of the Jura. The return of winter, which has so disheartened Paris, is welcomed by Geneva with opulent serenity. In this hotel the boilers have been rekindled and, in addition to the central heating, parabolical radiators have been installed in every corner, in much the same way that amateur gardeners can't see a gap in their rockery without popping in a fern frond or saxifrage.

Yet no feigned apostasy on the part of hoary winter can outwit or discourage the Judas trees, the double cherries, the lilacs of every hue, by this time obstinately set on their forward course. The start once made, they will sleep out of doors and bloom. Another denial of winter rises at dusk, from the peacefully dormant and rarely sluiced mud at the bottom of the lake. Throughout my wheel-chair perambulations I have to hold my nose against its floating sickly-sweet fragrances. Not enough salt in it. Your true-born Genevan, on the other hand, will sigh in ecstasy "Oh, that smell from the lake! It brings tears to my eyes, each time it comes back to me after I've been away." The green vein of the Rhône, flowing in at great depth, refuses to mingle with the common eddies, and cleaves its forceful path through the waters of Lac Léman, to escape, stabbed by the golden darts of the sun at its zenith.

The sparrow, that perky pedestrian! I had not intended to speak of it. I wished simply to give it food, and leave things at that. But in Geneva the town sparrow takes the initiative and can teach me a thing or two, whether I like it or not. Generations of worthy citizens have gone to the making of generations of trustful birds.

YUMA CITY-COUNTY LIBRARY
YUMA, ARIZONA

B
Colette
c. 1

The French bookseller, only three steps away—five or six turns of the wheel to my mode of approach—has been quick to pick up the customs of the country. "When winter comes, we divide the birds between us," he told me, " not for the purpose of eating them, but to look after them. On a night of sudden sharp frost a few winters ago, I had to get out of bed to go and free a gull which had its legs trapped by the ice at the edge of the lake, right in front of my door, the poor thing! " I too am in his debt, for he brings my fare of second-hand books out on to the pavement when I am unable to put foot to the ground, and in a stage whisper promises me "a Peter Cheyney " for the following week. He knows that for all the long days of spring the nights are not so short as the sparrows make out.

I can put up with their chirping as well here as in the Palais-Royal, for its modulation is so limited that it does not always break into my dearly acquired morning sleep. But I did not foresee that at the hour when the immaculate waiter brings in my tray and pulls aside the curtains drawn across my open window, no, I had not foreseen that at that hour my eyes would light upon not the *entry* of the sparrows into my room, but their exit. Seven of them, the colour of mice, came out from under my bed and went to rejoin their cheeping friends on the little balcony.

From that day on, I had difficulty in following the course of their familiarity, their demands upon me, I should rather say. Their appetite is unrelenting rather than insatiable. Three female birds started a nursery on my balcony for their young who had already sprouted feathers but still gave a pretty good imitation of the shrill insistence and shiverings of famished fledglings.

Jeanne Loewer brought me, from the Chaux-de-Fonds, a large round loaf of stale bread for the early morning regimental breakfast. The minute spindle-shaped females held their own against the round-breasted and better feathered cocks, their cheeks and wing plumage coquettishly marked. From watching them I have come to learn a little about that stranger, the bird, telling myself that, given four legs, it would look far more arresting than it does with its two wings crossed over its back, like Napoleon.

The mock-mahogany moulding at the foot of my bed later served as a perch for these lickspittle beggars who outstared me, bombarded me with their sharp, impatient calls and caught bread-crumbs thrown to them as would a French bull-dog. No sooner had I shut myself in the bathroom than they protested in increasing numbers that I should open the door again. The culmination came during siesta-time one warm and fleecy afternoon, when I became aware of some unusual movement close beside me, yet one that touched my heart. I found a pair of them, one close against the other, in a fold of the bed-spread. In an access of bliss, my effort to lean over them must have made too sudden a stir, for away they flew. This gave me fair warning that the time was not far off when I should discover one individual among their small, indefinite band, the particular one, the one who preferred me and was mine by preference. With the animal world, we are subject to the same perils every time. To choose, to be chosen, to love: the very next moment we are beset by anxiety, the danger of loss, and the fear of spreading regret. What an array of big words when the subject is but a sparrow! Yes, a sparrow. In love, there is never a question of smallness.

In the closing days of April, prior to the cold snap, "the darling buds of May" and the kerria were setting an example in their whites and yellows to the roses of summer, and the first gentians, down from their mountain fastnesses to the florists, were refreshing themselves in my tooth-glass, their stalks on a pad of damp moss, which helps the flowers to drink. Their sole beauty lies in their uncompromising azure blue; there must be some reason why we find ourselves so sensibly affected by blue! Age-old evocations of the firmament, a moist mirage in desert eyes, all that we hold to be eternal, is readily blue. The corolla of a gentian is tight-stretched on umbrella-ribs, the cordate cyclamen leaf is lined with mauve india-rubber: the edelweiss is pure cotton-wool. None of the three thereby loses its seductive charms and emblematic character of innocence. I am not forgetting that ubiquitous intruder, the narcissus! It is everywhere. Year after year it draws its devotees to Les Avants, where celebrations are held in its honour. And how do they honour the narcissus? By killing it. It is sacrificed by the million. Let us shed no tears, that's all it is good for. Once picked it is tied up in bunches that quickly wilt unless plunged into water. Its journey down from Les Avants by car, van or cycle, has steeped the road in unchecked, horizontally spreading scent, in the toils of which we first exclaimed "How divine!" then later "How nauseating!" Surely there can be few who are put off the lilac by its sovereign if funerary scent, the lilac

in any of its varieties, blue, purple or mauve, or the sparse
and delicate thyrsus of the Rouen lilac! My mother
"Sido" used to say of this *varin* variety "I can never
make up my mind whether its scent is rather nice or perfectly horrid!"

In many a plot the cherry trees here have overtopped
the walls or spread beyond the party hedges. Green yesterday, the fruit is ruddy today, and tomorrow will be
ruddier, rounder, heavier still. It acquires an even coating
of red, almost glazed, and then it is tempting to eye,
mouth and hand. Stretch out an arm, and it is mine,
yours, ours for the picking. I pass the trees every day, and
I notice that never a cherry is missing. In my part of
France, a good shaking was just as likely to drop an
urchin hidden in the branches as a good shower of
cherries. "You cannot tempt the Devil," the pilferer
might plead in self defence, cherries in his mouth and
cherries in his pockets. In Switzerland, as I have told you,
they have no devil.

III

I HAVE received a love letter: *"Madame Colette, I adore you! I am a very handsome fellow. If you will not say me nay, I shall pay you a call and give you a kiss on the nose."* It was signed " Béni ". I did not care to throw away my last chance of having an affectionate interview with a Prince-at-the-very-least-oriental.

He came, attended by a female slave who called herself his mistress. He evinced no disdain when treading the worn carpet of my hotel bedroom, and to start with my dearest friend and I did not know what to say to him; but he was not put out by our lack of words, nor did this deprive him of his princely expression of friendliness.

He was rose-pink—as indeed those Persians known as " Cream " should be when without blemish and, as was this gentleman, loaded with honours, medals and First Prizes. He was almost copper pink, his front paws not a far remove from the good earth, but rising in tone towards the tail. Clad like a fairy, he seemed miraculously at ease in the midst of a cloud of fur that beat against his sides at every step, and provided him at the back with breeches of insubstantial fluff. His coat was a profusion of clustered curls on chest and belly, and escaped from either ear in feathery tufts.

I hesitate to speak of his eyes, not knowing how to

capture their exact shape, the wide gleam in them of liquid gold and amber, the calm confidence with which they returned our gaze, and their latent smile, the outcome of a petted childhood. Round his nostrils too was the bloom of the same rare shade of copper pink.

To increase our speechless adoration, he spoke. The voice of the Angora is ordinarily soft and low, without prejudicing their amative periods when they are changed into howling demons. He jumped on to my quaking knees and, since he had promised it, gave me a kiss on the nose. He was pleased to display symptoms of curiosity about my bathroom and over the cheeky sparrows on the balcony, to whom he delivered a pithy address in the tremulous tones that inform the feathered race of the exact sentiments of a cat towards them. Wanting for nothing, he was without covetous desires, and when we saw him turn away from the birds to go in chase of a ball of crumpled paper, we uttered cries of delighted affection.

I held him for a moment in a tight embrace, tufted and sweet-smelling as a bunch of flowers. He gave me another kiss or two, on the tip of my nose and under my ear, and all the while his slave was expatiating on his noble lineage and the fruits of victory he brought back from every competition. She added a few relevant details: "He is unmatched for cleanliness; he not only puts up with but actually insists on his daily toilet with brush and comb; if at times it is his pleasure to show signs of abject submission, the slightest reprimand will cut him to the quick and may even ruin his appetite." I took solemn note of these "light touches" that added authenticity to his portrait; I transcribe them here in a suitably genteel tone.

Anything to do with cats, in my thoughts or in my writing, must never be treated with banter.

The musical ear of a cat clearly differentiates between familiarity and affection. It was not merely from her delight in playful fantasy that the Last Cat enjoyed my " Cat, come here at once! Cat, go to bed! " that formed part of the evening ritual. Gaily she scampered away, racing to her basket, and giving a passable imitation of a dog obeying orders. But it is true that the cat prefers the intonations of the human voice which come nearest to singing. In my few remarks to " Béni ", I observed the essential protocol. All the more since, to his other perfections, was added that childlike air of majesty which Angoras are slow to discard. Far removed from his character were the depth and intensity of the Last Cat, with her too ready aptitude to feel and express grief. For instance the year when, rather against her better nature and following a brief encounter with the shoeblack on the corner, the black and white bistro cat, and the grocer's small ginger, she produced a fine bastard daughter, striped, smiling, and half-witted, that we called Jantille. At once the Cat drove her from sight and affection out of pure jealousy, so much so that the very name of Jantille on the lips of either one of us would evoke from her a feeble little anguished cry. So we gave Jantille away as a present to the Curé of Mesnuls, and the Cat's aggrieved heart found peace.

It is to " Béni " that I owe this retrospective daydream. His resplendent presence, memories of the Last Cat, whatever acts as a touchstone to renew or remind me of cat personalities or cat characters, at once takes me back to a past climate that used to be both poignant and essential, but has since been renounced by me, prudently and with detachment.

Béni, for his part, seemed desirous of going to sleep on my knees, over which was draped my soft vicuna rug. He had already settled down to a rippling purr when his mood changed and, starting to mew in a minor key, he led his slave towards the door. The princely visit was ending with the end of his patience, the short-lived, brittle patience of the feline species that suddenly snaps and makes as putty in a man's hands the trained lion, the broken-spirited tiger in its cage, and the puma sulking in tears!

Amiable still, though distant, Béni made short shrift of farewell courtesies. He even rebuffed me with his soft cat's paw, conditioned by custom to gentleness yet ready to remind me that, dormant in their sheath—indubitably pink—it held sharp-pointed claws.

On my outings I drive along at the leisurely pace of a lady of the Second Empire. A pony-chaise could overtake me. There is always so much to look at when one travels slowly. Contrasting beauties effaced by speed fall into their proper perspective. My years and infirmities have surely earned me the right to go slow, to stop at whim beside a narcissus, a purple orchis, or a wild strawberry! No need now for my dearest friend, while at the wheel, his chin jutting out like a radiator cap, to interfere with his "No, no! No wild lavender, no honeysuckle, no cytisus! No time for a snack before Saulieu! You'll make havoc of all my timetables!" Nowadays it is he who picks my wild hyacinths for me. In the long run there is something to be said for having arthritis.

Thus my stoppings and startings become voyages of discovery; I go from garden-restaurant to riverside garden, I take stock of bowers and arbours and rose gardens. Here the municipal gardeners are busy planting out the roses they have kept hidden off-stage by the thousand. Roses assume a military elegance when paraded in serried ranks. As we pass them by, certain precocious battalions salute us with the special scent of their species, the unmistakable breath of "tea" and "tea hybrids". How quickly they go—how quickly am I going! Yet an aged body like mine clings fast to the winter of its discontent and its attendant ills, wraps itself up in shawls and rugs, derives a secret satisfaction from the chilly aftermath of the doctor's visit, profits from the anticipated loss of strength to withdraw into itself, and forget the spring. It is not possible to deny the spring. On a clear day the lake, though niggardly with indigo, might well be the Mediterranean. Children spangle the town with their little check dresses; grown-up girls go about bare-legged. Luxury is manifest in the spotless garment, the constant laundering, the fluffy jumpers that are the envy of Paris. And what a fine display of heads of hair, with never any need for the horrible "hair-pad"! Resplendent but not too feminine angels boldly fend their way through the peak-hour crowds, their hair a torch, their bare knees like glazed, crackling fruit skins.

I admire, I rejoice, I get about, I come into contact with all these long-legged Atalantas whose praises I sing— oh no, a thousand times no, don't run away with the idea that I am jealous, or sad! Do me the honour of believing

that I do know how to make the most of what is left me
of my part, do know how to bear lightly what would have
seemed heavy in days gone by, and derive from the flaw
by which metaphorically I am ploughed and furrowed a
certain . . . yes, I shall say it . . . a certain nobleness of
spirit. I hesitate before putting down such an expression,
sounding it out, taking its measure: what if it be too
grand for me! Believe, at any rate, that I have no need
for all the consideration I receive, that I laugh inwardly
when the kind-hearted, on my behalf, go as far as to use
the word "asceticism", as though it were a fitting rank
or title. Does anyone suppose that it would be easy to
escape the clutches of asceticism!

Will the various remedies which the Good-bye-till-
tomorrow-Doctor inflicts on me one day become a source
of amusement? One of them is greasy and glacial. Another
is more penetrating, has more quills than a sea-urchin.
There is yet another, which the body, stunned at receiving
so many steel-pointed light rays, cannot help but question.

Here I am, with two months all but gone, longing to
drink a toast to what the future holds in store for me of
the unpromised and unknown. Dear-Doctor-till-tomor-
row, I suffer from hope, and from modesty, and I ask you
as few questions as I can. After the time of roses in their
ordered ranks comes, I know, the symmetrical blaze of
geraniums, of scarlet salvias, and then will come the
dahlias, and later the chrysanthemums. Let us look no
further. While resting on shores made to bloom under
civic control, I have entered again into close friendship
with all the wild flowers of the Swiss meadows, which
are brought in to the proprietress of this hotel swathed
in a tangle of nondescript greenery. They come into my

room only after they have been sorted out, picked over and tastefully arranged by her own hands. Here the funny little face of some labiate nibbles at the wing of a bee-orchis—the fringed carmine beards of the ragged-robin emerge from a blue foundation of self-heal—the golden buttons of ranunculus from meadow and stream are wreathed in the insubstantial mist of their umbels—the three "Pasque flowers", mauve, violet and white, form the gauzy edging of a large, shallow bowl filled with lilies of the valley, the last of the season—already, a suspicion of baldness silvers the crimson clover. The crimson clover already! Have I then sacrificed, aided and abetted by my dearest friend, almost the quarter of one year to ministrations of which I cannot yet compute the range or the rewards, let alone alleviation? Not a soul has mentioned a possible cure to me, yet a constant appeal is made to my moral resources. Splendid! Least said soonest mended! In any case, there are so many methods of cure —perhaps I may invent one myself. To a dash of daring add a moderate dose of arbitrariness, a liberal dose of astonishment, much after the fashion of that ingenious child who stretched a piece of stuff over two rods set crosswise at the end of a stick and shouted "Maman, do look, I've just invented the umbrella! "

✍️ IV *Paris*

THIS year, next year, some time, never! When shall
we acquire what we most want, some of us poor folk
who are almost at the end of our tether, pent within the
four walls of a room, wedged between desk and book-
case, assailed by the footfall on the floor above and the
clatter of wooden soles on the staircase without? Not
tomorrow, not this year, will Paris provide us with one
or two " Gardens for Adults ". That the most pressing
need takes precedence, that first there must be " Gardens
for Children ", I do not dispute. And where can a large
enough site be found? I am not to be taken in by small
talk of that nature: when Paris requires a vacant site, she
finds one. Not without first looking for it, I agree. After
which they might very well endow a site for V.I.P.s. The
garden of the Palais-Royal is the very thing for such persons. It holds few attractions for children, who have done
it infinite hurt by their presence and their games. Sand
and gravel are non-existant, the earth has been stamped
into insensibility, and it is forbidden to water the soil—
the lawns and flowerbeds alone are entitled to have their
thirst quenched, and the gardener tends these lovingly—
what we call our " Court " has to rest content solely with
the slow and time-honoured impregnations from showers

33

of rain, urine of dogs, and human excrement—let me put
"children's droppings", to make it sound better.

Here all is an open stage, where the principal players
are the children. Many are charming, most are gifted
with remarkable agility. The thin-bodied outstrip the
more robust. Their skill in throwing and catching a ball
holds my attention as keenly as a sporting event. At my
window yesterday, a Sunday, I was fascinated by a baby
girl of four or so, squat for her age, who was disporting
herself in the sabbatical silence with two male members
of her family, her father and uncle no doubt. This child
so intent on her outdoor sport repaid all the attention I
bestowed on her, so deft was she at stopping the ball with
her foot, at throwing it back straight—and with either
hand—so adept at falling bare-legged and bare-armed on
the hard ground without a word of complaint. But, as I
could well see, she was an exception, as are child prodigies
on the stage or in the circus, so much so that when told to
do so she sat down in the wind and the sun and stayed
still like an athlete. And like an athlete she had put on
flesh : her face was a good colour, but far from improved
by two strands of plaited hair scragged back over each
ear and tied with a tag of ribbon. An exception, but a
welcome exception, formed by discipline and self-confidence. It would have been beyond the comprehension,
and envy, of most of our Palais-Royal children, that a
small girl of four, from some sense of quasi-professional
pride, could be capable of behaving with such zest and
restraint.

Not all the scenes beneath my window are as pleasant
to watch as that. Into my magnificent quadrangle seethe
a hotch-potch of young people all full of beans who, since

the war, intolerable and intolerant, have cast off the shackles of restraint and guidance. Quick on their feet but not fleet-footed, for their steps are conditioned by the imperfections of shoes no longer made to fit, they hop-and-go-one as sylphs might hobble if shod. Smitten from early youth with a passion for every sort of competitive game, like born neuropaths they follow their bent with uninhibited disregard for convention: they are true children of Paris.

In our royal enclosure we have never enjoyed any greater hygienic comfort and convenience than Versailles could boast under Le Grand Roi. Apart from the plush and luxury of the Restaurant Véfour and the amenities of the neighbouring theatre, there is not a single *buen-retiro* in sight. La Civette, to the greater glory of My Lady Nicotine, has pulled down its time-honoured mahogany stalls, which venerable dames used to tend with such care. Of what matter is that to the Garden's imperious guests, the children? When the need comes upon them, down slip the little shorts and up go the little skirts and . . . There are even simpler methods still. The infant in arms will pipe up from its pram with a cry of alarm; without rising from her wrought-iron chair, that indestructible relic of past ages, the mother or watcher will snatch it up and hold it at arms' length, as though it were a strainer of liquids and solids! Yesterday, immediately below my window, nine little puddle-stains all along the stone flags testified to the fact that among the chairs that afternoon nine children had slept, taken food, and . . . evacuated Oh, what malodorous incense rises in the evening air!

The war and its aftermath conditioned our children to jungle practices. A few days ago I saw two bigger boys of about twelve coming my way. They stopped at the first tree on the Valois side of the pleached alley. I thought to myself 'They're going to micturate in unison '—we're quite accustomed to that—' against one of those old decaying trees that never quite die.' Not at all. Lowering their already man's-size trousers, they jointly deposited the copious insignia of their brief visit. Throughout the operation they chatted amicably, without bravado and without shame. Shame and shamelessness mean nothing to them. But since it was broad daylight the passers-by, for their part, did look the other way.

With a child, making a nuisance of itself is instinctive and terrifyingly ingenious. The appetite for destruction—in other words, invention—has to be satisfied when and where it can. The return of spring sees the pink chestnut candelabra cut to shreds by the stone-throwers, and brings back the stalkers-on-the-slates so skilled in dislodging at one fell blow the nests full of young birds from under the ceilings of the arcade.

A generation of disheartened parents confront the children of today. It would be easy for me to fill these pages with shameful tales of child hucksters, schoolboy gangsters, striplings who act as stooges for big-time criminals: in short, of children who have never known the joys of childhood. Will they, perhaps—in the words of Labiche—come to know childhood in old age?

But I haven't the heart to curse them, my lively sparrows intoxicated by their own chirrupings, my whistling little cobras, my embryo artillerymen, corn-crake-voiced chatterboxes and maniac trumpeters, all the more because I have never lost either the memory or the benefits of a parental upbringing which instructed me in silence before all else. I cannot spend my time abusing them, because I observe them and by observation make them my own. I do not lay claim to them in the name of a pseudo-maternity which has never come easily to me, but from my window above I recognise in them my own blood, my own race, my own past, my own faults, whether reclaimed by time or aggravated by age. Ideal greed that feeds on fancy! This naughty child secretly belongs to me, as the animal with whom I exchange some sign of recognition is mine, as one of the plants in the flower-bed is mine since I am perhaps the only one to know its name: *penstemon*. When I passed on this name to another citizeness of the Palais-Royal I received in exchange a brief shrug and for answer "Don't make me laugh! How can I believe a name like that!" I was in half a mind to take her up: "You don't want it? Then give it me back. I shall share it only with M. Henri, the gardener, who loves his flower-beds." And having classified it among the objects of my ideal possessions, along with my fillies, my newly hatched chicks, all the marvellous offspring of my own modest phantasmagoria, I shall put the *penstemon* to much the same use as did Théophile Gautier the flower of his imagination, the *angsoka*.

✐ V Beaujolais 1947

WHAT a fierce, unparalleled, interminable summer
this has been, rising again and again from its ashes,
converting Normandy into a parched Ardèche, Burgundy
into a waste of esparto-grass, laying bare and dry the beds
of all the mountain torrents, as well as the bottom mud of
ponds where frogs expired and fish lay gasping! Only
now, when the time has come round for the nights to turn
cold, can a good word be put in for the fearful summer,
responsible as it was for so many of our food shortages.
In no sense to restore it to grace and favour, for it is
past redemption. Its savagery began at dawn, with the
animals athirst and all the herbivores deprived of sus-
tenance. You might see a man using only one small
watering-can to sprinkle a cabbage field, one of those
huge fields that in good years do honour to the outskirts
of a town, a single man among ten thousand yellowing
cabbages. You might see a cow that, while pulling up the
stubble blade by blade, had swallowed ten kilos of earth
and died of it. You might see . . .

No, I shall never be able to link together a series of
agreeable memories with the aid of such pictures. They
blacken and reduce to cinders my favourite pastime of
day-dreaming for pleasure. Forty-one degrees centigrade
in Rue de Beaujolais at noon, and thirty-seven at two

o'clock in the morning: how far away it all seems now
when, through my high half-open windows, the December air forces a vertical passage, whitened by fine frozen
snow which, for a brief moment, wreathes with a halo my
blue lantern that burns by night and by day. A few
seconds are sufficient for the cold to take possession of
my room. Quick! Now's the moment—without making
a physical movement of any kind—to plunge back into
whatever of the summer's bounty was least harsh and
dehydrated, there to discover something to make the
mouth water, to bring colour to hand and dress, something pertaining to freshets and dew: let us return to the
brief recompense, all the more real in that it was un-
solicited, granted me at the fiercest moment of the
ferocious summer: vintage time on the slopes of Brouilly.

Most certainly, for an arthritic like myself, the worst
is not the getting about from place to place, always provided that the journey is made by car. The worst is taking
ten steps across the room, walking five yards along the
garden, having my night's rest broken by sudden, sharp
jabbing thrusts of pain, reaching out with the quick,
impulsive gesture of youth in an attempt to pick up my
stick or lift down a book—oh, how inveterate is youth,
its agility now purely of the mind, and chastised the
moment it strains at the leash! As for the stairs, their
descent is now a matter of humiliation and guile: for
when a stranger passes, do I not stop and, standing still,
pretend to be putting on a glove or fumbling in my bag!
Once the stranger is safely out of the way, I laugh at
myself and my old woman's wiles.

But put me into a car, with a cushion here and a
cushion there, and away we go! You won't hear another

word from me for a prolonged stretch of miles. In bygone days it was the Cat who decided, by a yawn of hunger or some discomfort of the bladder, the spot where our Ark should come to rest. She ate little on a journey, and feared travel sickness. A nip at Saulieu, a lap at Vienne, with a refresher of grass between times. My requirements are on a less modest scale than hers. When she was of the company, we hardly had time to finish our woodland picnic before she demanded to be back in "her" car to smooth every hair of her coat, blue as a storm cloud coming up from the west.

As I was saying—saying to myself, rather, though I was committing it to paper—it was a masterful decision on the part of my dearest friend that got me away, as he alone knew how, at crack of dawn on a morning that reeked of heatwave, melting asphalt and dried-up river beds, set on a course for the slopes that border the Rhône. There the small tight-bunched grapes are less decorative than the opulent Provençal muscat, that trails its six-pound allurements under the vine-stock and offers its fresh-skinned belly to the lizard.

What benefits could I hope to reap from the Beaujolais vintage? The never varying torrid heat, my very helplessness, everything seemed fated to keep me apart from such a rough and rustic festival. I would have been content to listen to the sounds with which it covered the hills, the wains creaking along the rough tracks beside which I took my morning nap. Voices hazy with early morning fatigue arose from the heights of a neighbouring vineyard and then declined, descending ever lower as the sun rose higher. I could picture the slow work of picking, the baskets filled, the increasingly parched throats of any who thought to slake their thirst by biting into a bunch. I kept the persistent summer at bay on the far side of closed Venetian blinds, on the side of the flaming ball of fire, the flies, the demented wasps, and the dusty mint plants, the side on which could be viewed a glint of a dazzling fragment of the Saône as it sparkled in the valley, far away. I exercised a modicum of patience. I listened to the red-tailed wall-creepers rustling the ivy above the fountain and cutting the thread of its jet.

But better things were in store for me. Friendship can achieve much. A chain of linked arms settled me in the car one day, and in the recesses of one of his private chambers, I bearded My Lord Wine, whose threshold I had thought never to pass.

He received me in the cool bosom of a hill without my having to put foot to the ground. It was I, seated in my chariot, who had the air of a conqueror. With its great door thrown back, his Palace had the appearance of a sequestered grotto, and from its spacious ceiling he enveloped me at one and the same time in an icy cope of motionless air, the divine and mushy odour of crushed grapes, and the droning hum of their fermentation. Lamps shone like twinkling stars along vaults a hundred metres in length; vats spumed long thinning festoons of rosy froth over their sides; a team of dappled horses, blue-tinted in the half-light, were nonchalantly munching grapes that had tumbled to the floor; emanations from the new wine, heavy, impure and but newly born, blended with the steam rising from the sodden horses.

A sparkle of ruby red flickered over the chased ribs and bosses of a silver cup which, at the end of an unseen arm, a man's hand flourished in front of me: " A forty-four in its prime, Madame. But come back and taste the forty-seven when the time comes round! It will be more than the equal of this."

Come back! How probable, how easy this sounded as I held the cold rim of the brimming cup between my lips, under the arching grotto that barred ingress to the heat outside!

As those about me were of the opinion that the *grand vin*, the starry cavern, and the shade of the hillside tunnel could perhaps be considered as antidotes, we made another trip, this time by night, taking another route to climb another slope. This time the shade was provided by a wistaria that clung to all four sides of a courtyard; issuing from a single trunk, like a huge writhing python, it rose hugely to heights where it became lost in its own foliage. The covered-in courtyard, lit by arc-lamps, rang with the clangor of voices, wheels and heavily shod feet, for the forty or so vintagers of the estate were on their way down to their repast, bringing in with them their aroma of male vigour and the juices of the vine. How dearly I should have loved to follow them down! Our cold collation on the ground floor was a feast of ham liberally padded with fat, sausages that had a whiff of new harness, and a special cheese, called " strong ", that provokes an unquenchable thirst.

All honour to labour where honour is due: below stairs, the forty vintagers were to sit down to the better table, consisting of omelettes, pork, veal and poultry, washed down with a wine which, like the finest rubies when held to the light, keeps the clear brilliance of its generous, full-blooded colour.

The fatigue that follows a faultless meal, served with

a young vintage wine on a summer night with no dewfall, can be agreeable enough, provided it is not forced or prolonged. In the court-yard at the time of our departure, under the swinging arc-lamps, the huge wistaria coiled its living spirals. But, since we were the first to leave, I could not appreciate any but the sharpest sounds emerging from the great silence that little by little was settling over the hillface: flights of brittle-winged elytrons jarring against the standard lamps at the entrance; the hoof-beats of an unharnessed horse clattering along a cross-road and, above all, soft music on the ear, invisible and held in reverence by all, the never failing babble of the freshet, the last, this fevered year, where gasping hill and parched dale could slake their thirst.

VI

FARGUE and I, confined to our respective beds, used to talk on the telephone. Not very often, but at considerable length. I dearly loved, and shall always love, his fat, rich, infinitely elastic voice, with a shade of suffocation over it caused by chronic bronchitis. My memory bears me out that our verbal exchanges were never anything but affectionate, frivolous, riddled with news of our work or of our leisure, and of course with every kind of reminiscence.

I was always curious to learn from him the manner of his suffering and the nature of his physical pain. "Today it's hammers, yesterday I was in the grip of a vice, a sort of continual grinding," he would say, and then go on to question me about my periods of sleep and sleeplessness, but I knew full well that he was reproaching me for my failure to sound romantic: whereas in his mouth an ostentatious choice of words would throw a glamour over his very disea^re. . . . I shall make time and space to talk further of him, as he used to be.

When he allowed me into his house to see his " Family Portraits all hung on the line," I had good reason to show my delight and gratitude. Thereafter I wanted to see more and more of him. I wanted Fargue both in the flesh and in the mind's eye, Fargue traipsing across Lipp,

44

Fargue strolling down the street with his soft, untiring tread, and above all I wanted to see Fargue. Arrangements were made for my transference one day last summer, I being the lesser sufferer of the two. The first stage by car, through the streets at dusk on a fine evening—the streets of Paris, Fargue's undisputed kingdom, glittering with gold-dust, rich with his insults and charm of manner—a journey at whose end I knew him to be waiting for me.

At the Rue du Montparnesse end they bundled me into the luggage-lift sprinkled with coal. The ascent brought me to Fargue. Some whim or other prompted him to be found seated at table, so that I might think him capable of rising at any given moment, I can only suppose, to offer me his arm and bring me to rest at his table.

Six guests all told; but as how many should I reckon Léon-Paul Fargue, presiding like a Buddha, with all his eloquence and gaiety? He was at his best that evening, to the extent of giving reassurance to Goudeket and myself. I won't swear that he deceived our friends Doctor Martha Lamy and Professor Paulette Gauthier-Villars and even Chériane herself. But he made a good meal, scolded and laughed as scornfully as an intolerant prince. He complained of the too blue blueness of his sheets, and depicted for us what he alone could see. He talked to the cat, affectionately, for the cat was as glossy, as dark and beautiful as Chériane. Facing me was a portrait of her, large and striking, prominent and lifelike as a guest at table. To my right the ledge of the open window cut off the trunks of the plane trees; the lover of the streets had his lodgings among the branches.

I can find nothing to say about this last evening that is either more, or less, deserving of report, of regret, or of being affectionately preserved in the memory of his friends. No single one of us, not even Fargue himself, rose to the occasion. None of us felt either the need or desire to applaud, to make an occasion of it, or to register exceptional surprise. But I know that the six guests have not forgotten a single moment of it, that in the bitter certainty of there being no next time, we, his faithful and unfortunate friends, all feel ourselves to be the poorer.

I have not been to the theatre since I went to see *La Folle de Chaillot*. Not that I have not wanted to go; but, as Pauline says, " it creates too much of a song and dance " to get me comfortably installed in a theatre or cinema. Helplessness breeds timidity. I do not mean to say that it leads one to self-indulgence. Abstinence surely does not ruin the stomach for every kind of relish! In consideration of the length of time that one or two of my senses had been deprived of gratification, I should have expected the more readily available appeal to the ear and the delights and surprises offered to the eye to have given me a rejuvenated enthusiasm. And yet there I sat as wary as when I was a dramatic critic. I had hoped to be more agreeably surprised.

On the first encounter the shock was agreeable enough : the auditorium of the Athénée, encrusted with glittering gilt. Meretricious but magnificent! What a wealth of golden fruit and swags, with as many breasts as apples, as many pears as garlands and thighs! An auditorium for a real theatre, a real auditorium for a theatre, where Bérard's rollicking blues and reds were set off by a long lustreless black figure, the figure of Jouvet standing out against the set, Jouvet with jet sewn into his black tights, a long black exclamation mark!

Last night I committed the downright folly of re-reading *Le Festin de Pierre,* the cause of my considerable embarrassment in listening to the piece. It was like listening to a musical composition with the score open on my knees. All the same I was able to enjoy unreservedly my right to give no opinion. If I were forced to form a judgment on Don Juan as played by an actor who " walks off with ", after a line or two and a couple of capers, a pair of country wenches, I should find it hard to scrap my own conception of Don Juan as sombre, self-willed—I was about to write " abstemious "—endowed with that deep-rooted misogyny which women find so attractive.

This was by no means the first time I had been tempted by Don Juan. I had dealings with him in *Le pur et l'impur,* but not at any great length and only perfunctorily. I had forgotten about Molière and how little he knew about the subject, even less than myself, since it was not enough for him that his hero should have sinned against love. The reason was that treason to love was still beyond the philosophy of his day.

The play moves along, now slap-dash, now strait-laced, dealing harshly with the heretic and driving the seducer to insult religion no less than paternal authority: I should say that we help it on its way by our strained attention— I pride myself on being one of the best audiences I know —embellished as it is with too ingenious dramatic refinements. But how good it was in those surroundings! How they foster unreality! Balconies, mouldings, ceilings, a riot of reds and gold. I had only to lean forward in my stage box to touch the strutting actors with my hand; not one of them was perfect, not one could act badly if he tried. Two or three of them gave me a furtive greeting, a glance of recognition that took them momentarily out of their pretended character.

Outside the Paris rain teemed down in buckets and through it I had to pass to regain my refuge from wind and rain. A strong arm was at hand to give its unfailing support. In the thick of the crowd I knew I should again succumb to the timidity that afflicts cripples, for it is real and obliging pity that they most fear. In the time it took to cross the pavement and enter the car, I should be soaked like all the others, overjoyed like everyone else at having been to the theatre for a Sunday matinée, richer by my store of living images, and busy for the rest of the day with what was not my business but my concern, namely, the art and effort of others, and dearer still—for mistakes are more intelligible than success—the intelligent mistakes of others.

They invaded my room, each an exceptional personality, all three of them so vigorously present and alive, taking up so much space yet never encumbering a room little more than exiguous, the one sitting himself down on the prow of my raft and the other two where best they could.

They came in with their strongly defined characteristics written all over them. Yvonne de Bray, and her warm, well-bred cordiality; Jean Marais, nicknamed Jeannot, with his crest of hair and his irreproachably irregular features; and the young woman who, as recompense for having her face laid bare from ear to tip of nose, from chin to forehead, every line removed from her cheeks and thus rendered glossy as a wet-glazed jar, had suddenly become beautiful enough to play Beauty herself. Heavens! I was forgetting the dog, the dog Moulouk, who owed allegiance to one person only, to Jean Marais. Yet all the time we were together I hardly had cause to remember him; he faded into Jean's shadow, became part of Jean, took the form now of an armchair-leg, now of a small Persian rug, and up to the moment of their departure called no attention to himself, except when earlier in the proceedings he paid a visit to my bathroom on his own initiative.

"What are you looking for?" Jean asked him in an aside.

"A bidet, to drink from," answered the dog.

"To the left," I told him, "behind the bath. The tap's running, and there's always enough water in the pan for you to have a drink."

"Good," said Moulouk, "I'll find it all right, I'm neither deaf nor blind. Plock, plock, plock, plock . . . There's the proof."

Once more he parted the curtains with his wet muzzle and lay down again like a sack of nuts, emitting a sigh, for he could tell from the pitch of our voices that the visit was by no means over and that no one was going to utter the prophetic word. Indeed, our conversation was bright and far-ranging as we touched on this and that; we even rehearsed—at least they did—some scenes from *Chéri*, for a radio programme. For myself, I was perfectly content to watch them, while listening to their voices was an unearned increment. Of the three, Yvonne de Bray's affected me the most nearly. From time to time, when she was made to feel hurt, it would grate on a more enforced register with the insistence of an engraver intent on his block. The actress seemed impelled by some sort of modesty to carry simplicity to excess; she introduced the tone of a family conversation to one particular scene, and broke into a sob as into a gale of laughter. Unexpected inflexions I had not indicated in the text would bring home her words to an unseeing audience. An actress so pre-eminently endowed—and one so totally disinterested —should have it in her to play all rôles.

Turning my attention away from Yvonne, I followed "Jeannot", who diminished his huge bulk, his strong arms, and his strong legs trained to grip the flanks of film mustangs, to the dimensions required for Chéri.

Jean Marais play Chéri! And why not? In his author's conception of him, Chéri never had any traits in common with Musset's wan Lorenzaccio. And for a born actor what a challenge it is, and a rewarding one at that, to discover the means so to expand and contract his physique that a puny man can turn himself into a lusty athlete and a strapping fellow get inside the shell of a shrimp! The hardest thing of all for Jean Marais, if he is to play Chéri, will be to make temporary surrender of his natural innocence. He can at need make himself ugly, as in the part of the "Beast" (though in that film the grandeur of despair was hardly ugliness), but where will he go to for cunning, for soft-spoken insolence and a talent for falsehood, for the barefaced pleasure of failing, and of recovering only to fail again? For the moment I dreamt, as I listened to him, of seeing him on the stage. I could well imagine that it was his innocence, like a nugget of gold, that choked his big, fierce voice. Time will show. There is no hurry. For the present my three interpreters, who were close beside me where I lay in bed, were not playing what I had written, but playing with it. They were gay with the gaiety of beings whose life has one end, one vision, one light, and reckons on a succession of incarnations. They possessed talent enough to throw off time and again the watch on themselves which impedes the inferior artist. "*Nounoune chérie! Nounoune chérie!*", faltered Jean Marais. Nobody had asked of him a stage performance for the radio, yet he collapsed into the arms of Yvonne de Bray, who all at once found strength enough to support and cradle the weight of an athlete. "*Mon méchant—Ma beauté—Te voilà——*". Jeannot made himself hoarse with sobbing, as required; the dazzling blue eyes of Yvonne de Bray, as they gazed at him, were moist with tears. Was all that for me, the solitary spectator? I was under no illusion; it was all for themselves, and, in their own despite, for honour's sake.

Of course I have one, like you, like the rest of the world; but if I never let on, nobody would ever know about it, so discreet am I in my use of it. At this moment it is softly murmuring to me one of Violetta's great arias, the heroine of *La Traviata*.

That full credit may go to the soprano, the accompaniment is a mere poum, poum, poum—poum, poum, poum, in three-time. The *diva* takes advantage of this to do full justice to her soprano voice, but she is not too much for me; for I have moderated the tone, and the sound of my tiny American machine, of an apparent capacity of about a cubic decimetre, does not penetrate beyond the closed door of my room.

What must be must be. After going all through my cupboard of gramophone records, and finding it full to overflowing, I gave them away, and kept only "The Cat's Aria", an American number which really did make my unforgettable Cat smile. Later on, when a bad illness took the Cat from me, I smashed the record, preferring silence, preferring above all the talent of those compassionately rich and generous people who would sit down at our "cottage" piano: Poulenc, with "Jean Hou-Hou" and *Les Animaux modèles*, Jean-Michel Damase, with his flexible voice, in our *Rouge-gorge* and our *Perle égarée*.

After that we sold the piano to buy a book-case! One memorable day my dearest friend brought home the smallest—but is there not always a smaller than the smallest?—American radio set (no aerial required), which sang all the way up my staircase. We deposited it on my divan-bad, where it started to give a spirited rendering of *L'Enfant et les Sortilèges*: "All you have left me is a single golden hair, like a moonbeam on my shoulder". Ever since then, it and I have been boon companions. I tone down the great voice inside the body of a dwarf, I employ its ventriloquial gifts as much on Trénet as on Beethoven, and I do not overlook its great virtues on account of its small failings.

I am too antediluvian ever to lose entirely my earliest memory and sense of the miraculous when in the presence of a radio set. How splendid that children the world over can be on terms of intimacy with this polyphonic prodigy! In whatever outdated year was it that I visited, at the invitation of General Ferrier, a hall dominated from floor to ceiling by a vast frame—hexagonal, as far as I can remember—seemingly held together by strands of green silk? If I am not mistaken, the contraption swerved round vertically on one of its sides, giving out a confusion of sounds; these were explained by General Ferrier as coming from various points of origin, for he was a great expert in this rapidly evolving invention which was already one of the world's new wonders.

From within the six sides of this harp and from behind the long strands of green silk, there suddenly came to us the song, far away and limpid, for which one bird alone could be responsible. But someone said " That's Constantinople ". Not a soul dared show surprise at this intelligence, for such was the immediacy of our new emotion that a nightingale heard in Paris could not but be oriental, by the same token that a flying carpet is oriental, that the moon is crescent as it rides on high above the silvery Bosphorous.

VII

"*THIS village where we live, set about with woods
and a dark fir plantation, is where I teach the
village children of twelve and thirteen, telling them of
your mother, Madame, and how she would taste before
dawn the forbidden fruits of her household chores.* I
teach them to know, which is to say to love. If ever, in
the course of your existence, no bonds of vassalage have
bound you to any overlord . . ."*

There I stop, before I quote the whole letter, and
because it concerns only myself, the writer and his office
to the young. Surely this one passage is sufficient to give
more than an inkling that its author is adept at turning a
phrase! How delightfully we obscure denizens of the
French countryside can express ourselves when we have
a mind to it! I say "we" by reason of the pride I feel
in belonging, as regards both native land and love of
style in writing, to the same race as my unknown correspondent. He, as he tells us, is a village schoolmaster.
Lucky village! Above all, lucky children, who can with
confidence entrust themselves to such a guide! I hesitate
to write "lucky teacher", unless he is enabled to rise
above the rigours of his profession by some especial saint-
liness that exalts his loneliness and pride. This man has
written to me in his native tongue whose crystal purity

* See *My Mother's House*, pp. 129-30. English ed. Secker & Warburg.

54

he exemplifies, being himself passionately devoted to reading, and a contemplatist; he has written to me and shows surprise that I have sent him an answer. The children in his school have also written to me. Using coloured pencils, one has drawn a flower, another a house, and a third, having also drawn a dwelling, tells me " what cannot be seen " on the other side of it. But I have no difficulty in realising what he himself sees there—the garden, two fir trees, and a lawn. When one is twelve, it is easy to see through walls.

The worthy schoolmaster is not my only correspondent. I also receive letters from schoolmistresses, some of whom love to write for the sake of writing, others with a genius for inventing games and other ingenious ploys, who are clever in winning from an unresponsive child the word or smile indicative of so many pledges, so many conquests. Then, in the hour of their success, to whom are they going to relate it? To me. You can well believe, for one day at least, I am filled with pride.

Madame Wattine has sent me a parcel of cornel berries. The good old French name for them is *macres*, or water-caltrops. But cornel sounds more horny, and has the tang of her rural Poix. Water caltrops are so little known, so unappreciated, and last so short a time, being considered a delicacy only in districts where there are ponds, that I should like to say something about them. My appetite for them is as strong as ever. To prise them open I had to make use of one of the stone stairs in the house where I was born. For this strange water fruit, of ooze and autumn bred, forms with its four protective horns

when fully ripe a shell of very hard texture, definitely
"Chinese" in shape according to Fix-Masseau, and the
method prescribed, first to avoid cutting oneself and
second to lose nothing of its mealy kernel, is one scoop
with a practised hand, a good stout knife, and the step
of a stone staircase. In return for which you will acquire
blue-black stains, a couple of damaged fingers, and an
attack of marsh fever into the bargain if, as I used to do
and am still capable of doing, you eat some four hundred
caltrops straight off the reel.

"And . . . are they really good?" I am asked by
friends deep-dyed with incredulity and circumspection.

I thereupon assume a dreamy, sentimental, and slightly
stupid look, in fact become very like the little girl I used
to be, and answer "I don't rightly know, but I happen
to love them."

Indeed, I know nothing to compare with the taste of
these water chestnuts,

> *Prickly, tickling chestnuts,*
> *Which tickle the thighs,*
> *And prick in the pocket,*

as the solitary caltrop-vendor, sack slung over shoulder,
used to cry up and down the streets of Saint-Sauveur. At
four sous a hundred, and he gave good measure!

The caltrop, or water chestnut, has a bluish white flesh
the consistency of a wax candle and a kernel which, like
its husk, is neither almond-shaped nor spherical; more-
over it neither looks like a chestnut nor does it taste like
one. Even when cooked it still calls to mind the pond
where it was born and the mud that nurtured it. Its long
tubular stalks—the root-stock vegetates in the slime—

crisscross the bottom mud before rising to the surface, there to disseminate their delightful white flowers, flat leaves, and later the drab green fruit so quick to sprout horns. If not gathered in the nick of time, the fruit will detach itself from the tubular stalk and sink back to the murky depths, to settle down beside the small tench of which, to my way of thinking, it bears a distinct flavour. The following year it will be its turn to sprout and direct the gradual ascent of sleek leaves and white flowers at the end of a pliant tube.

On my ponds an old punt puts out here and there to gather the water caltrops during September-October. Or else a man, nearly always an old man, clad in the remnants of a tattered pair of breeches, will kick off his sabots on the bank before wading breast-high into water that has ever a treacherous appearance, inasmuch as it rises from latent springs in rippling wavelets of alternating warm and cold currents, and is the habitat of little else than stout undulating water weeds that elude one's grasp.

The fragrance of riverside reeds, of spearmint, of eddying, disturbed water mingled with the parlous and pervasive savour of caltrops, these delights are not yet destined to escape, not for this year at any rate, one who has the wits to keep them safe in her Paris room—by denomination a writer increasingly under the dominance of her malady, but each day afforded relief by the faithful memory of her brain and of her subtle senses that in old age have lost none of their cunning.

In anticipation of the time when I shall no longer be able to move, I make no effort to move.

I ride at anchor beneath the blue lantern, which is quite simply a powerful commercial lamp at the end of a lengthy extensible arm, fitted with a blue bulb and a blue paper shade. Though a permanent fixture, it has none the less suggested to my neighbours the name they have chosen to baptise it with—*fanal*—the light that rakes the seas. "Madame Colette, you can't imagine how pretty your lantern looked yesterday, shining through the fog. . . . Oh, but you can't tell me that you make sparing use of your blue lantern! It's on at all hours, in the early morning, at eight, sometimes at seven-thirty even!" There is nothing I can hide from them, not even the moment—at cock-crow, perhaps—when the beam from my lantern casts a blueness over the brown coffee-pot and the white milk-jug. I tend to make less and less distinction between the hours of night and the hours of day, the hour for reading, for writing, for looking about me, all are equally good. The hour for conjecture, for testing my memory! Before long I shall be confusing the hour for work with the hour for conjecture; wondering what Gide can be up to—my enticing Gide, whom I can never see enough or read enough—and fussing over some crazy scheme of mine, will become one and the same concern. One good example of a crazy scheme was my longing to copy the lovely rug which Jean Cocteau had bought for his house in the country. All of a sudden I felt I must have it! But the rug was at Milly! I must have it, I have to have it at once, so I summon it by telephone. I am answered by a chorus of voices: my neighbours in Rue Montpensier become alarmed; Jean Cocteau has been called abroad, Jean Marais is on some film location or other! What matter! Paul-of-the-bookshop (easier to pro-

nounce than Paul Morihien) shall be dispatched to Milly,
they'll charter an aeroplane, they'll send the Emperor
of the Indies!

At that point I begged that nobody be put to any
trouble, insisted that there was no real urgency. Too late:
the wheels had been set in motion on my behalf from
Beaujolais to Montpensier. Then out of the blue Jean
Marais sprang to life before my very eyes, tall enough to
brush the ceiling with his orange—no, moonlight blue—
no, auburn mop of hair! And what in the world was he
trailing along behind him, slung from his shoulder? It
looked like some long drag-net.

"Have you come straight in here from a fishing expedition, Jeannot? Sardines, is it, you have there? Or
good fresh herring?

"Nothing of the sort, it's *the* rug. Nobody could find
the time to go to Milly, Jean's somewhere up in the air
between Paris and New York, Paul-of-the-bookshop is
busy arranging some book exhibition, so off I hopped
there."

A hop of one hundred and twenty kilometres, there
and back. He certainly had lost no time, with his seven-
league boots. In everything about him there was an air
of breath-taking efficiency in carrying out an indisputably
urgent commission, in his white rain-coat, his turquoise
blue cashmere scarf, his hair rising straight off his head,
and the panting mask of his dog Moulouk. How was it
possible to confess to Jean Marais that it would not have
mattered in the least if nobody had gone to Milly! What
reverberated throughout my little room to the exclusion
of all else was this haste of his, and in my imagination
the sound of the full-tilt gallop along the road, the kid-

napping of the rug, my staircase scaled as readily as the
stairs of a convent thrown open to the Musketeers! Jean
Marais, Jean Marais, hero of countless films and plays,
how admirably your legend fits you, and how splendidly
you live up to it! I told myself that day that I had seen
you playing the lead in *The House of the Fisherman,*
and that in your wake trailed the drag-net, bringing in
with it the smell of seaweed and the glitter of a myriad
opalescent fish scales!

From time to time I have to take stock of what has been
going on in the world of the cinema, so I do go to one
film a year, or two. It is not sufficient. But it is enough
for me, once I have settled down again to the rhythm, to
the black and white of the screen, to find myself
astounded at how much there remains of crude ostenta-
tion and simple incongruity in the realm of cinematic
invention and representation. After an enforced absence
over lengthy periods, I ache to say to the screen " Don't
tell me that you are still where you were! What have you
been doing whilst I've been away? " And then I allow
myself to fall under its spell once again. It is so hard to
withhold one's admiration. I forget that we have every
right to demand colour and " audience participation ",
and in the end I am content to go away with what I have
retained of my journey to the other side of the world,
of the human conflict, and of my own insatiable curiosity.
Happy come, happy go, like the roan mare in the story
books.

They (the Radiodiffusion people) one day asked Jean Cocteau and myself to record a short conversation in which "we could say what we liked", and "promptly" the radio van arrived outside, and "promptly" Jean was here beside me, perched on the poop of my workaday raft, with the rays of my blue lantern turning his face green.

This culmination of happy coincidences did not prevent Jean and myself from exchanging a glance or two. I was quick to catch the look of apprehension in his deep-set eyes that he must have been aware of in my own. We had to improvise, and I am no good at improvisation. And I feel far from at home with that bell-shaped flower, the campanula—pear, cucumber, or whatever name it goes by —which an insidious hand was already holding out toward us. Too late in life I came into contact with the microphone, with all its paraphernalia that climbs in through the windows, sprawls across the kitchen floor, strangles a small table in its progress down the passage, and coils up close beside me as I lie in bed.

" And how do you feel about it, Jean? "

" Me! I have an unholy horror of the contraption. And at the present moment I'm asleep on my feet. Ever since noon yesterday I've been hard at work, right on through till one o'clock today. What's more, I've had no proper lunch. I'd far rather speak to a thousand faces and a thousand pairs of ears than into this . . . this pumpkin! At last—is all set now? "

" All's ready."

" Then you'd better begin. What are we going to talk about? "

"Anything you like," proposed the young man in charge of the coils.

"But I don't like. So you begin. Suppose we pretend to be taking a stroll in the Garden? "

"On my crippled legs! You make me laugh."

But I was not laughing. Neither was Jean Cocteau. He closed his eyes, hid his face behind his long elegant fingers, and courageously launched forth. I was full of admiration for his diction, his well-timed periods, the variety in tone of this musician-orator. I responded as best I could, but my best was not very good. However, the young man with the campanula was pleased to give us a " perfect! " before he rolled up his coils, detached himself from his calix, and made off, while I pulled back my bench-table close beside me with the crook of my harpoon-stick. Under the stress of emotion Jean's face had gone black and blue under the eyes, and I quickly withdrew my still icy hand from his. We lost no time in concealing our attack of radio fright. I believe mine must have been the worse, since it forecast a whole host of other pitfalls. It gave me advance warning of the voice sticking in the throat, the speck of dust in the tonsils, the unexpected spoonerism. In vain it inveighed against the major betrayal: for it is all very well, but I have never in my life spoken in such a deep cavernous voice like the one I heard, I have never arrrticulated in such an ultrrra-Burrr-gundian manner! People assure me that I am mistaken, that my voice comes over on the radio just as it sounds in " real life ". I shall not dispute the point.

Jean Cocteau comes into my room, and I look at the

time by my cardiac watch, and am amazed: eleven-thirty
in the morning! Had it been at night I should have had
no cause for surprise. Before I can ask any questions he
supplies the answer.

"Yes . . . Can you believe it, but my electricians,
camera-men, and carpenters in the studio have just told
me they're on strike!"

He contrives to squeeze his long body on to the poop
of my raft, folds his arms and legs, and coils up his body
so as to expose as much as possible of it to my sun-ray,
which will shortly be coming up to noon.

"So what?"

"So nothing. I walked out of the studio."

"A holiday! Calm yourself. It's always like that."

His nose looks at me sideways, in some perplexity.

"To be strictly accurate, it's no longer like that. I've
worked like a mad thing for a number of years now.
Night, and day, and Sundays. On a tray, on a restaurant
table, on the grass in the country, on paper. In the past
it was the pressure of work that half-murdered me. Today,
I no longer know how to knock off work unless a break
has been arranged for me well in advance. Once again
I'm being deprived of my poison, and I'm aching in every
joint. It's a quarter to twelve. I'm not hungry. I never
feel hungry. What is there to do at a quarter to twelve,
when one's not working. I've forgotten."

"Stay here with me."

"That I can't do. Stay here with you at a quarter to
twelve! It's simply not done."

"Where will you go, then?"

"To be honest, I don't know. I'm going to try to go
home."

From the tone in which he says this, he might be embarking on some great adventure.

As the wind was coming from the right quarter, I could hear the bells for the midnight mass; then, a little later, I listened on the radio to the mass by J. S. Bach. Pauline had elected to go to Saint-Eustache, whence she returned disappointed. "The crowd was far too great and it was perishing cold. And it wasn't a proper Market crowd. For me, midnight mass must be made up of Market people." On this sibylline utterance she left the room, to see the New Year in off Auvergne cheese and a pint of champagne. I could not have chosen better myself, had I felt the least bit hungry. But I simply had no appetite for such a repast, no more than I used to have, it must be added, for my old pre-war New Year's Eve revels. How many were the *Réveillons* in the good old days that found us grouped together in some famous restaurant—the men in white ties, the women in low evening dresses—along with great editors-in-chief and big industrialists, even with deputies and ministers who considered themselves great!

We also used to see the New Year in at Madame Hessèle's among the notable artists of the day: Vuillard, Dunoyer de Segonzac, Luc-Albert Moreau and others. This was already an improvement, despite the early stages being a little too formal under the military discipline of our hostess, white-haired and dressed in white. She would have reminded us of Madame Aubernon, had that good lady not been so far removed from us. But what a lot of good painters there were to give full rein to their high spirits!

Elsewhere, in other studios, I remember how the furniture used to be moved out of and brought into the room to allow for table space for the oysters, the turkey, and the foie gras. The first wave of champagne was rough and far too cold, the second already too warm. The *consommé en tasses* was too clear, the caviar too black.

In every restaurant little multicoloured cotton balls, guarantees of reckless gaiety, began to rain down as soon as the soup came in, and into the soup, as often as not! Oh, I have a store of memories of even more enjoyable réveillons! But tonight they are dormant, and I am lying down.

A tour of my quarter, by car. Apart from the butchers' shops, apart from the silver paper and the apples, I search in vain for the quondam opulence of the *premier arondissement*. Once again I find, and can still appreciate, the stylishness with which—fine artists that they are—the gentlemen of the butchers' shops dress their meat. As he chops, cuts, slices, trims, shapes, or threads through the string, a butcher is as good a sight to watch as a dancer or mime. A Parisian butcher, that goes without saying. With his golden bang of hair atop his forehead, his cheek ruddy as the dawn and his ear pink as a rose, with his apron strings tied in the approved style and spotted here and there with just the proper amount of blood-stains, I can tell you, Madame, that a Parisian butcher is well worth your passing glance; worth more, perhaps, than that.

My promenade, were I to allow myself to make one, would turn into a melancholy pilgrimage. In Rue de

Valois, under a lovely balcony, that famous restaurant of old—*Au Bœuf à la Mode*—used to hold sway. Today the balcony is still there. The succulent beef, the excellent way of making sauces, of cooking carrots, bacon, and calves' foot, are no more.

> *Irai-je voir le bœuf gras?*
> *Irai-je voir ma maîtresse?*
> *D'un côté l'amour me presse.*
> *Mais le bœuf a tant d'appas!*

Did Gavarni himself compose that quatrain? It appears as the caption to one of his enchanting drawings, in which he has grouped a posse of "Lions", excessively tight-waisted, and ladies of the town, with sloping shoulders like Rhenish wine bottles and dark Andalusian eyes.

Next door to the *Bœuf*, let a tear be shed for the *Pâtisserie Flammang*, famed for its éclairs and Neapolitan ices, and for the departed glories of its glass panelling of the Restoration period, painted with garlands. The Flammangs were reduced to penury by selling their delicate cream-tarts and puff-pastries which simply ran away with the best butter.

I mourn the loss of the good proprietors themselves as much as that of their good confectionery. All among the flowered panels, as pleasing to the eye as those of the Grand Véfour, lived a family of ladies in black, the eldest of whom had her place at the desk. A younger sister supervised the faultless service of the waitresses, while a second generation, represented by a young woman of unobtrusive colouring, enquired after the health of the customers as she wrapped up a tartlet, a *saint-honoré*, or a *savarin*—"Deliciously moist, is it not, Madame?"—in its conical tent of tissue-paper. A little girl who never opened her mouth made out fair copies of the bills close beside the cash desk. Flammang's is now a co-op painted in bright green. The ravishing glass panels have found their way to the Carnavalet Museum. A fat lot of good that will do us—and them!

All of which is none too cheerful. If I failed to stand up for myself, I should become as grumpy as any old dotard. But I do stand up for myself, I do myself well on the black market. I go gadding off to a shop in my wheelchair, a place known only to myself and a few others and presided over by a dazzling young lady. For nowadays you will no longer find "black" establishments run by tight-lipped shrews or gruff, sardonic young persons. Cordiality is now the order of the day. As to its whereabouts, you had far better make enquiries from Simone Berrian, or Cécile Sorel, but do not expect me to reveal to you the spot where I was once lost in admiration of the pair of them, each as agile as the other, perched like a couple of wagtails atop precipitous chests, plunging their hands into dingy drawers as though they were branpies, from which with shrieks of triumph they fished out a varied booty of mealy camemberts, a small bag of rancid nuts, a pair of espadrilles, a powdery cake of Marseilles soap, as well as other treasure-trove which they seemed to value far in excess of its true worth and utility. To such a pitch, that at one moment, like birds gorged on a surfeit of black currants, they neglected to notice, from their perch on high, what a fine display of their pretty legs they were exhibiting. None of this was lost on a young man, the apparent owner of the store, whose looks betrayed his feelings, the entire stock of his sentiments. But for him I should never have realised how disinterested the running of a black market business can become, as much under the influence of passion as of nameless reverie!

But here I am speaking of times past and gone: all the actors on that particular stage must long since have returned to the paths of legitimate trading—all, that is, save myself.

 VIII

28 January, 1948.

IN the room which no device could ever sufficiently heat
I was born laboriously on January the 28th, 1873, and
I caused my mother much pain in her travail. For close
on forty-eight hours she struggled as only women in the
pangs of childbirth know how to fight. The women about
her lost their heads and forgot to feed the fire in the grate.
By dint of her cries and anguish my mother drove me
from her womb, but since I had entered the world blue
and silent, nobody thought it worth while to bother about
me.

There was very little of charm or comfort about that
room. Curtains of flowered print, mounted on an old-
fashioned triangular frame, were draped over the widely
separated beds of my parents. A curious little squat boot-
cupboard stood in the embrasure of the window opening
on the street and could be used as a seat. The glass-
fronted wardrobe of three unequal sections was made
of Brazilian rosewood, lined with polished thuya, and
always struck me as over-decorative and out of place.

The twenty-eighth of January came and went fifteen
times without witnessing any change in the room where I
was born half-choked, but showing a determined will to
live and even to live long, for I have just reached my
seventy-fifth birthday—an anniversary the friends around

me persist in calling "a great day". It is they, let me say, who have made it so. They have given me so many things.

They have given me flowers, fruits and sweets, and offered their congratulations on my seventy-five years from morn till eve. They have eulogised me in the papers, to an extent that has led me to think that I have nothing but friends in the world. They have sent me letters and telegrams and photographs: "You can see how pretty our little girl is at three months! We have called her Françoise." And a sheaf of picture-postcards! "Madame, this is simply a little Swiss cat wishing you a happy birthday; she is seven months old and quite white." To which, kitten or pretty poppet, the palm?

They have sent me the first violet of the year: "Jacqueline had the idea of going to see whether there was not one in flower under the sheltered briar, and such enough there was one!"

Anacreon (Richard) has written to me: "Since there are not seventy-five candles in our house, nor in the whole Rue de Seine, I am sending you seventy-five carnations, one for each year."

A bottle from Bordeaux has travelled all the way here in safety, bearing on its little paunch its vintage year—1873, the year of my birth—and its cobweb of precious dust. Like me, it was kept on its back till dinner-time on the twenty-eighth of January; again like me, bless me if it hadn't retained something of its fire and colour, together with a pleasant suspicion of violets, and the Mouton wine which it brought me was sleeping peacefully on its bed of lees, from which we awakened it with care and gratitude! And my dearest friend put a circlet of gold round my wrist—my favourite metal whether it comes in the shape of a bracelet, a medal, or the links of a chain. There were many other presents too, fit between them all to choke me with emotion; there was the blue-black hyacinth embroidered on a gilt-edged card, and the pink hyacinth from Rosa, and the snowdrops from two little working-girls, who did not leave their names and made off at once; a splendid array of fruit from Pauline: " I could not have borne to let anyone else give Madame finer fruit, today of all days! " There was the spray of orchids from my daughter.

" I bet it must have cost you your shirt to buy me this spray! "

" Oh, no Maman, don't you worry. You know perfectly well I never wear a shirt."

And from my neighbours there were flowers without end for my small vases, as well as a painting of a rose by Redouté, and a wonderful sausage of purest pork for cooking.

And two American ladies have put in my hands two of those American parcels, one from the East and one from the West, which gladden the eyes no less than the palate; for the silver paper, glazed cartons, flowered wrappings, and glossy containers double the attraction of the plums, gâteaux, pure wheaten flour, Malaga grapes and the transparent sweetmeats they contain.

" I'll swap my share of powdered milk for your empty box," was the offer made to his sister by a little boy paying me a neighbourly visit.

" Don't be silly! I'm not such a fool," answered his sister. " Not even if you throw in your mint chocolates as well! "

And then the full jereboam of champagne that I had!

And the zariba of red azaleas raised all round me by my fellow members of the Académie Goncourt! And the newspapers splashed with affectionately possessive references to "Our Colette"! How I enjoy being a joint estate! Marguerite Moreno's warm voice spoke to me on the radio, borne over the air on its incomparable rhythm, rich in a great variety of overtones, with every now and then an accent of affection and tenderness—at the very moment when I was not listening. Marguerite did her best to console me for not having heard her: "It makes no difference, ma Colette. We'll have a repeat performance, you and I, in seventy-five years' time." Oh, Marguerite, I would like it well enough at this moment, now, when I know what it would be like, when to my divan-raft, loaded down with presents and lit by a blue lantern, I have welcomed a disorderly array, such warmth and affection, and a wealth of smiles and tears not unworthy of youth itself.

Only a very small remnant of the younger generation of my sex can nowadays be numbered among my intimates. I should have more, if I let them come. But I dread them. It is in the course of nature for declining strength to be scared of up-and-coming new forces. Severity in passing judgment on the latter is not the former's lot, even supposing we possessed it.

The cocksure approach employed by the very young to hurt our feelings will always be quicker off the mark than our judicial utterances whenever we attempt, unsuccessfully, to temper enthusiasm by a little fairness.

I have never suffered from lack of curiosity. Why

should I go to the lengths, then, in face of the young of either sex, of denying the attraction that other forms of first appearances hold for me?

Curiosity is seldom a root cause of ill will, yet how is one to make best use of it once the days of temperamental effrontery are behind one? I have no fear of my women friends; but I fear a friend's daughter, even more so the daughter of a friend's daughter. The children who do not come to see me but who write me letters lay claim to great timidity. If they mean timidity about literary matters, which may lead them to seek advice and tips, I can well believe them. But as to timidity of other kinds, it is for me and those of my age to feel it, almost to the point of painful intensity.

I do not go out of my way to offer encouragement to my youthful friends. I do not go so far as to drive them away. They must find me lacking in conversation, since the truth is that for them I have very little to give, and I am left with nothing but a consuming itch to ask questions when I take a hand in the most exhausting of all pleasures. When I am alone with those already settled in a profession, I never end without winning from them what I best like, something of the romance of their profession. I like it the more for the fact that they do not seem to realise how moving they are when giving expression to their hopes and fears. Their pathos emerges, wrapped up as it is in the most commonplace expressions our language contains, in expletives, in hideously accurate computations voiced without a trace of emotion. Yet between them and me stretches an ever widening and worsening gulf, unbridgeable by friendly familiarity and still less by expressions of good will, in which they have but little belief. Curiosity—which in their self-infatuation they consider fair enough—serves my turn better, as does that mischievous gift for reading the heart, inherited from Sido, to which I have playful recourse. I make only playful use of it, never in the spirit of triumph. Let me stress that for all my advanced years some of my amusements are perfectly innocent.

My youthful girl friends and I find it easier to cope with topics uninvolved with intimacy, such as the theatre and its concern with dramatic art, the cinema as a means of getting on in the world, bibliophily considered as a business opening. In these fields of human activity, they beat me hands down. Young people of both sexes know all there is to know about these everyday outlets. The pleasure I derive from being astonished fills them with pride and makes them talkative; what is more, both sexes turn out to be on common ground in their pursuit of special editions, autographs and dedications, in their passion for "Grangerising" or extra-illustrating "original issues", to the neglect of fine old albums bound with a clasp-lock, and other "Golden Treasuries". Crazes of this sort are curiously interrelated with a strong family feeling, long thought to be a thing of the past; not long ago I signed a copy of *Le pur et l'impur* presented to me by a bibliophile aged five-and-a-half, whose far-sighted mother had brought him along for the purpose.

In so far as I can make contact with such remote creatures, I find our young French girls to be lively and ambitious, but troubled in mind. Their self-confidence is merely a façade. They are mettlesome but quickly discouraged, like draught-horses that are not properly fed. They bear the traces of an inner conflict that has barely troubled their conscience, as it were a painless wound. Among my acquaintances are three sisters and a female cousin. One of them has devoted herself to music, in spite of all and in her own despite, and nothing will induce her to give it up. When music decides . . . Another paints, but before another year is out will not, I believe, still be painting. The third is a dancer, and every day grows thinner. A question of good beefsteak, this!

The female cousin has snatched at a small opening on the stage, and is shortly to make her début in a piece in which all the characters are eighteen-year-olds; meanwhile she is doing, as the saying goes, "a spot of filming". She does not say "a spot", however, but "a sport", being still child enough to enjoy the language of mystery.

Her name is Catherine. Were she not called Catherine, her name would be Chantal, or Dominique. Her parents are lacking in originality, foresight, and historical sense. She comes to see me because her mother, who is only twenty years younger than myself, says to her at intervals: "Go and pay a call on Madame Colette, be very polite to her and do not tire her out."

"Can I ask her to put in a good word for me with Jean Cocteau?" asks Catherine insidiously.

"Yes, but make it sound as if it came quite naturally into the course of the conversation."

That only goes to show that Catherine has been well brought up. She comes into my room and, before untying under her chin the scarf which makes a hat unnecessary and keeps a permanent wave unruffled, she will say "Madame Colette, would you be so kind as to say a word for me to Jean Cocteau?"

"Yes, if you will tell me about the dress you are to wear in the first act of your forthcoming play."

"The dresses for it are excellent, as is always the case," she obliges with a specious air of condescension. "If I get nothing worse than a 'sport of bad news' in the papers from Jean-Jacques Gautier, I'll be able to live that down. Especially as my dress in the first act is in a ribbed aquamarine ottoman silk. A small bunch of mauve auriculas at the waist and a great white forehead."

"A great white what?"

"White forehead."

"Where on earth . . ."

"Why, on the forehead."

"You've not got a vast forehead, thank the Lord."

"Oh, I'll enlarge it with an electric razor!"

"How horrible!"

"It's indispensable. It's the hallmark of purity, especially in the case of a *jeune fille*. Besides everyone—every woman, that is—has a great white forehead."

"I am only too well aware of it. And 'on the day' you will also, I suppose, display in all their nakedness the little bare bumps behind your ears?"

"Why, of course!"

"Indecency can go no further. Have you never looked in a glass to see the back of your ears? In which case don't you know that even in the prettiest woman, or the prettiest child, they are a plague spot? That ever since little girls have had their hair screwed up into two tight-plaited pigtails, like lobsters' tails, they have looked hideous in back view? That behind the ears, napes, and children's skinny necks, are places in the process of formation that should be kept hidden by a providential growth of vegetation, light, golden or brown? That ever since women took to sporting what Marguerite Moreno calls 'the vast encyclopedic forehead of a waiter' compatability has ceased to be possible between your face and the hazardous frivolity of your hats, between the desert of forehead and the neat wavy garland that sweeps back off it, between the barren earth and the bird perched above it, between the blasted heath and the arch features of a girl of eighteen like you? "

"There is nothing arch about me," Catherine interrupted stiffly. "And it was Jouvet himself who once told me that my future lay in wronged women."

"Jouvet and his wronged women! That may be . . ."

"Oh! " Catherine began, blushing with expectancy.

But with a gesture I cut short her budding and evident hopes. "That is not a promise, Catherine. Go on! "

"But so far I've told you nothing."

So irreproachable a repartee, so just a criticism of my flow of words, laid me flat. A very palpable hit!

"There is still some Swiss chocolate left in that box, so do help yourself. What's new in town? "

"That the fringe is coming back into favour. Very soon we shall all be looking like Lautrecs. You'll like that, Madame Colette! "

I turned on her the glowering eye of an old warrior and deluged her with a shower of truisms dear to my heart, touching on the comparison of a head of hair to foliage, and the female face to fruit; I even went so far, to put Catherine on her mettle, as to bring to her notice the superb, curl-bedecked, young foreheads of Martine Rouchard and Dominique Blanchar. A moment later I was in full cry as I recalled the raven kiss-curls that so enhanced the wan and cat-like face of Rachilde. And I had good reason, for Catherine was looking at the time by my cardiac watch. Her sole reaction was to banish from her face every hair that had strayed from her ash-blonde tresses with a thoroughness which might have been taken for an impertinence, to excuse herself on the grounds of " her " rehearsal, and make an effective exit, after an " au revoir " very prettily mimed and spoken, the *sine qua non* of good manners, as they are called. As if good manners turned on a gesture and an intonation! This fair-haired, sharp-angled Catherine intimidates me, but I make an impression on her.

She did not take her leave before offering to help me: " The rug? Your cushions? Are the sticks within your reach? " A fresh-cheeked girl, sophisticated, hard as nails, courageous, wrapped up in herself, and perhaps, in her heart of hearts, a romantic. I like the element of contradiction in her, her pleasantly acid personality, the rebellious spirit in so young a bud. It seemed to me that once man—the hand, the mouth, the body of a man—had touched her, the world around her would be aware of it . . . myself the first, naturally. Was I like that, I wonder, at her age! My memory is not clear, but I vividly recall my shudder of repugnance when I was very young—does Catherine feel the same with me?—at the touch of old people, and the wild delight with which at the end of the visit I made good my escape from Mme de Cadalvène or Mme Bourgneuf, old ladies of over eighty, whom age and infirmity kept glued to the window panes on the well-worn rim of their constricted nests. I avoided the clutches of the small paralysed hand, crumpled as a claw, that offered me a stick of Vichy barley-sugar. It needed every ounce of Sido's authority to force me to pick up a detested silk scarf from beside a pair of lifeless feet shod in felt slippers. Equally detestable to me was a certain china cup, and also a certain cushion of black woven horsehair. . . . It was I, therefore, and not Catherine, who heard a quiet voice saying "You must be very kind to Mme Bourgneuf." But in those days I had eyes for details only, the very things that are now, inescapable as doom, gathering on every side of me, to wit the pair of crutches, the vicuna shawl, and my spectacles.

Oh . . . Pauline, fetch me quick my blue dressing-gown, yes, yes, the new one, and the rose-pink foulard, and the scent-spray, and the bowl of cyclamen from my table—my powder-box as well. I ought to have been given all that, goodness knows, just before my young visitor arrived. I look a perfect fright.

Rare are the days on which I receive no presents. Let us understand each other; I mean, almost exclusively, presents from those who know me well, and know how to cater for what I call my insatiable appetite. Today I have received the first chestnuts, small, hard, and dark brown, finished off with a broad, light birth-mark and three stiff little hairs at the tip, showing that they have only just reached maturity. They come from a wood quite close to Paris, some seven or eight kilometres away, which I can see from here: a steep, wooded slope, sparsely planted with ill-tended oak and fir and chestnut. A mere slit in the road beckons the passer-by, uninvitingly, to come upon a wooden chalet, set on brick-work that is losing all its mortar. What can this *dacha* be doing there? Hush! We must respect the cerebral repose of two over-worked doctors—" my doctors " I call them—who cut themselves off from the world on Sundays. On one occasion I was able to follow them into their retreat, where they gave proof of a blissful resemblance to all children who ever hid in a wood, lit a camp fire, ate off a paper plate, drank from the same bottle, and they listened to the silence perforated only by the whistle of a train and the twitter of a tomtit. Having tracked them to their lair but once, I know that squirrels frolic high above them and that one blazing hot day they covered the escape of a large grass snake. Their view consists of unpeopled tracts of the Ile-de-France and the surrounding countryside, both scoured by railway lines, both speckled with small villas, but serene and all the more expansive for the sky above them.

It is but seldom that I can accompany these two am-bitious women, who dream of putting behind them con-sulting room and laboratory for a few hours. Their several skills long since outdistanced what the untutored mind can grasp, yet they gaze in wonder at the mimetic spider simulating a pink pearl among the pink heather flowers, at the rotund puff-ball, that unspotted egg laid when the nights are freshening. They know what it is I long to see and bring it back to me: a hatful of ripening chestnuts and edible mushrooms, to appease my greed, and for my pleasure a variety of wild flowers, the matted head of the rose-gall, together with three unripe chestnuts, tight-packed in a single husk. The husk is beginning to split and through the cleavage can be seen the gleam of the three light mahogany fruits. By a trick of my peculiarly tenacious memory, I can close my hand over the ligneous twig-tip that held suspended this lovely green sea-urchin and then all I have to do is to clamber up as far as the solid wall of leaves to reach the neighbouring pines. Further on it is all sand, birch trees, heather and bramble-bushes laden with berries. Just let me go there, I shall not lose myself. Shut the door of my bedroom. I need nobody to guide me on my walk. All that I needed were these three chestnuts, packed tight in a single half-split-open husk. Au revoir, au revoir, I may be a little late for dinner.

Jean Marais has given me a landscape, painted in oils on a small panel. In the foreground, on the bark of a great branching tree, he has inscribed my name. Beyond this tree, the fields spread out and lose themselves in the distant sea near Arcachon, and on its azure blue I am lying.

The stage vies with the screen for the allegiance of this tall, stern-visaged archangel, and the stage is fighting a losing battle. To visit me he has to fold the wings he has battered against the sets and burnt in the " sunlights ". He does not complain, he calls his angelic patience into play. But often he tries to make good his escape. Some-times he succeeds, by availing himself of a little entresol tunnel with a very low ceiling. Sitting with knees up to his chin and elbows to his sides, stiff all over and happy, bent over a panel no bigger than a cigar box, he painted for me a splendid section of immensity. After which he came to give it me, embraced me, did not jar my crippled legs, did not upset my working-table, or send my spectacles flying. He shoved his forehead—his " Beast's " forehead—his tawny mane of hair and his puckered nostrils, between my ear and my shoulder, without in the least bit crushing me, expressing in a single caress affection and strength. Meanwhile at the back of my room Moulouk, who owns allegiance to Jean Marais alone, who ages when he is away and grows young under a look from his master, turned away his head and refused to say goodday to me.

Last week I became a receiver of stolen fruit. "A lady of my quarter" brought it me, speaking in a whisper but bubbling over with the story. A slightly wrinkled apple clung tenaciously to a bare twig in her hand. "It's a Japanese apple," the story-teller murmured. "It comes from the gardens at the foot of the Eiffel Tower. Somebody stole it for Madame Colette, just when the gardener was lighting his pipe." I gave myself up to an incontinent dream that the Tower Gardens, hitherto unexplored, were really a paradise of exotic trees given over to mango, cherimoya, or pineapple—perhaps, who can tell!—to the gigantic fruit of the jacquier.

For hardly had I got the apple to myself when it began to exhale a half quince, half apple odour which I can only qualify as Circean, enchanted and enchanting, and so potent that even the atmosphere in the next room—more often than not so redolent of fried onions—was cleansed by it. In a matter of minutes the stairwell, Mecca to their too assiduous lordships the tom cats, smelt of nothing but the strongest apples and quince mitigated by lemon juice, magnified twenty thousandfold, all three of them. Losing all sense of proportion, the fragrance continued on its way down to the ground floor, where it woke up the lady of the book shop who, two fingers to her dreamy forehead, took herself to task for having allowed her preserves to overcook.

When night fell I invited the stolen apple to sleep close beside me, in the embrasure of the window, for all that midnight and the waning moon might quadruple its propensities, and though my dearest friend from his adjoining room might try his best to dissuade me by crying aloud, calling down countless maledictions on Japan, apple-trees, the dangers of toxic exhalations, and pilferers from public gardens. But since he is well mannered enough never to raise his voice when driven to cry aloud, I did not hear him, and trustfully embarked on a wave of sleep almost immediately fraught with dreams and delusions such as had never before assailed me on my divan-raft.

Even then the last word was still left in dispute between myself and the origin of evil. Since the weather was clement for so late in the season and I was able to sleep "in the garden", I had only to make a long arm to take the apple in my hand and cast it forth. I then noticed through the balustrades of my window, for the garden below was already whitening with the dew at dawn, that a long cat had sprung out from the spindlewood hedge and was chasing after the apple. But no sooner had he caught up with it than he retched violently and at once began covering it over with earth, according it thus the fate it doubtless deserved as a fugitive from some dubious Eden. Then he made off with a cat's measured step, supposedly satisfied that he had exorcised the malignant spell by the potent means of ashes, vomit and oblivion.

I have long since discarded the habit of examining an envelope before opening it, or scrutinising the handwriting before perusing it. This habit persists only in the case of solitary persons, of those deprived of letter-writing friends. Too soon I took to massacring the envelopes, sometimes to the detriment of their contents. André Lecerf would tell me that herein lay a revealing feature of my character, but not, I fear, a very flattering one.

Why do I not make use of a paper-cutter, so much more convenient and more elegant? Ah, there's the rub! Why, among my total collection of paper-cutters, can I never find one to serve me faithfully? In the good old days I used to buy them ten or twelve at a time, of white wood, at station bookstalls. Thereafter they would disappear, all ten or twelve of them. The point of my pencil insists on breaking and flies up into my face. The pull or push-bell has become a stage accessory, a wire without a voice. My watch, as I have said, is cardiac. The evening paper simply melts away, disappears. All these are family misfortunes, and are hereditary; my father could only control the mad antics of *Le Temps* by sitting on it. What's more, the human paperweight was hardly adequate. What use do people find for a piece of india-rubber? Or for a ruler? The various chattels designed to make work easier have never stood me in good stead; but my form of spite, which is simply to do without them, has theirs beaten. I almost persuade myself that I am now in the course of achieving a measure of independence. And high time too! The times of postal deliveries are exciting moments indeed in a writer's life! Mangled the envelopes, lacerated the letters from strangers—oh, if only they wrote more briefly!—an unavowed appetite, the hunger for the society of one's fellows which makes one ask for more, plays havoc with their missives, and at the same time calls forth an "Ouf!" or "Is that all?" What is left of my interest in graphological studies leaves me grumbling and offended at the sight of certain handwriting. If every script paints a portrait, I object to each single written page bearing the speaking likeness of a disagreeable grimace.

Between the ages of six and nine, I wrote quickly and badly, as did all children who were taught only the slanting hand, called "English", which involved keeping the shoulders straight in line and the right index finger humped. About my thirteenth year, to my great good fortune, a lively, exacting young woman was promoted to the post of teacher in my village, who said, as she bent over my copy books, "Your handwriting is vile. Why?"

I was not expecting the final monosyllable and could think of nothing to say.

"Yes, why? Your writing is inexcusable. I give you a week in which to improve it. That's ample time. Take to using a Flamant No. 2. nib, which has a broad point. That will help you to form your letters slowly and clearly, and more upright. Has it never struck you that to be illegible is an act of grave discourtesy? I will not tolerate such an offence against myself."

The results of a wigging such as that were not slow in taking effect. Fifty years later I tried out a similar gambit on Claude Chauvière, whose handwriting positively repelled the reader. Flowing to the extent of being formless (a feature not, alas! without significance), negligent of loops and lines, omitting any couplings, her script was like a streaming banner struggling to free itself; to decipher it caused me as much annoyance as discomfort, so I treated Claude like a badly brought-up child.

Being both proud and quick-tempered, she went red and pale in turns. "Madame, I shall spare you the sight of my distasteful writing and the company of a person of no education!"

At that I called her a noodle, a word she drank in as the highest compliment, and her face suddenly dissolved in tears and laughter. Now I am very happy to come upon her and her careless hand once again, in the margins and the interlinings of that gale of exaltation and perplexity of soul which I have in proof and to which she gave the title *Manuscript found in a Monastery*.

The magnificent, harmonious handwriting of Germaine Beaumont brings cheer to eye and mind. In it can be seen and read all the vigorous merits of that great writer of fiction, and even one extra for good measure: I mean a sort of noble disdain, to which her talent, and the independence that she has won for herself, give her the right.

My own writing is not ugly, though I say it who shouldn't. It is like myself, a little stocky, the upstrokes full and rounded, and legible. I may as well pay myself a small compliment every now and again.

It is by no means easy to rid ourselves of the idea that the time of a postal delivery—especially the first morning delivery—is a time of hope, surprise, and reward. There is animosity in our love of the bundle of scribbled envelopes when still fastened down, then opened, then thrown away. We stop loving it as soon as it holds no more secrets, no more confidences, no more endearments, as soon as it becomes prolix, or degraded by consorting with prospectuses, advertisements for patent medicines, book catalogues and cards from galleries.

Our closest friends, when far removed from us, are the only ones who write us letters with a maximum of reserve and a minimum of news about themselves, remaining silent about their own troubles and concerned entirely with ours—let me particularise and say " with me " and my arthritis: they have discovered an osteopath who . . . a radiologist whom they . . . They quote the case of a miraculous cure, a thermal spring whose . . .

This has the immediate effect of bringing out the worst in my character, since I had anticipated reading an account of their journey, the events of their stay, the exact number of teeth cut by their small daughter, the exact height of the floods in their district—in short, their news. Have none of my friends, my dearest friend included, the least idea of what interests me?

I console myself with the remainder of my post—the letters written to me by strangers. Other than having the good luck to happen upon the peculiarly French grace of writing good letters, I may yet come upon something to astonish me. For people ask me for things which I had never supposed to be at all in my line, for instance " a trustworthy person who could look after a lady of advanced years ". And again ". . . if it is not an impertinence, a decent man, grocers' assistant type, who would accept comfortable post in a town of middling importance. I take the liberty of asking you this, Madame Colette, since everyone knows that you are renowned for your knowledge of the world."

Certainly, Madame! Perhaps not exactly to include the life of a grocer's assistant; but "everyone knows "—I like that "everyone" which gives me self-confidence—that a request for advice about the ailment of a pet does not frighten me, and that I do not throw into the waste-paper basket the story of the caged canaries, set free for reasons of economy, that became crossed with house sparrows and, two years later, are still producing offspring with a small yellow feather showing here and there in their plumage, and with the suggestion of a trill in their throats. I do not tear up the account of a domestic tabby who by dint of love and patience finally induced a handsome, suspicious wild cat, step by step, quivering with exhaustion, to enter the house in the woods. Nor do I throw away the drawings of children. If I were to follow my own inclinations, I would throw away nothing. I do my best to follow my own inclinations as little as possible and to husband my harsh words for anything evil that may come my way in search of strength and encouragement, for the momentary itch that goes by the name of vocation, for the proliferating novel, the literature that loses its way, and for bibliophily in its lazy and primitive form: "Madame, I am leaving my copy with you, and tomorrow I shall return to pick it up enriched by a dedication from yourself." You find the formula somewhat summary? I am not the author of it, I would have you know.

Not all the young bibliomaniacs are quite so . . . succinct. Are they mistaken in taking such liberties? Possibly, since once my initial fit of spleen against the hard, businesslike methods of youth is over, we sign, we respond! However cross they make us, we never feel we are entirely free or quit of them. A single start of refusal brings me up sharp before the most legitimate claim they have on us—the claim on what they call our experience. They need advice and criticism. They want, like my little Yniold, not only " to go and say something to some-body ", but to listen with attentive ear to a voice that will speak to them of themselves.

Children and young people, you who make bold to write to me and in the very first lines tell me of your "timidity ", have you never envisaged the possibility of my timidity being greater than your own? I seek protection, I remain silent, I fear you. I try, but without either naming you or betraying your confidence, to laugh you out of this crazy business of writing to an old woman as if she had no option but to perform a crazy act herself—answer you. Since I cannot do less, I read you, and with scrupulous care. But I have a well-founded suspicion that those who are worst afflicted with the itch to write are not the predestined favourites of literature. Yet to tell them as much . . . I feel that I have neither the right nor the inclination to do so!

Let us, if you will bear with me, read over together some of the shorter letters, which have to my ear an im-perturbable note of complacency and fruitless childishness about them. In the first one I catch an overtone of Marguerite Moreno and her businesslike method of answering letters, with something of her gentle raillery.

"Madame Colette, I am much inconvenienced by the death of Madame Moreno, since it has deprived me of the chance of meeting her. This lady had been very kind, she had promised to receive me and to give me favourable

*notices in the papers. For I have the gift of comic writing,
and people of my acquaintance tell me that my essays and
light verse are striking. One day when I telephoned Mme
Moreno, I told her that it would be advisable not to put
off publishing them too long since I am sixty-nine years
old; but she told me that, on the contrary my age would
be an additional attraction. Seeing that she has just died,
I take the liberty of addressing myself to you, etc.,
etc. . . ."*

*"Madame Colette, I wonder if you remember me!
When you were once staying at X, in 1904 it was, I was
the little girl of seven who used to run errands. Since that
time, I have married and we have suffered many misfortunes. Things are beginning to look up a bit, but we
are still wanting for a number of little things. So I
thought of you to write to, and if you know anyone who
would let us have for nothing a motor-car that is due to
be scrapped. My husband is very clever with his hands
and he would be sure to know how to make something
of it. Thanking you in advance, dear Madame Colette,
etc., etc. . . ."*

Another one? Let us take one more, in my opinion the
most unexpected of the lot.

*"Madame, I should like to put some of your writings
into verse, among them* La Maison de Claudine. *Spon-
taneously I make you this offer, to superimpose on your
rhythm my own strictly poetic versification.*
If, as I hope, you like this idea, perhaps you would

also like to write the preface? I should find your advice useful on a number of points (publisher, typeface, method of sale, and so on) . . . I enclose a few samples, which I consider representative of my work."

Believe it or not, these things do happen, just like that. In what spirit should letters of this kind be read? Is there anything to be found in them other than calm self-assurance, with above all an astounding ignorance of real life and, in contradistinction, the secret cult of the self and the crying need for publicity?

Would not you fall in love, as I do myself, with those who advise me for my good? Not all of them wish me well, but to one who lacks self-confidence, their assurance is like a slap on the back.

"Madame Colette, reading is our greatest pleasure; but we do not conceal from you the fact that we find your stories of days gone by a little fatiguing, we should prefer something more of our own day. We do not scruple to write to you, for what we have to say may be of some service to you, etc., etc. . . ."

"Madame Colette, my sister and I enjoyed reading your last book. Do, please, give us some more stories about your childhood, they are much the most amusing. As to your talks on the wireless, you ought not to read them out as you do; you should talk naturally, as though you were having a conversation with yourself, etc., etc. . . ."

" Your ' Souvenirs' are a bit colourless, a bit lacking in go. What is required is more emotion, more tenderness, in your dialogues with your dearest friend. On the one hand too lifeless, on the other too literary, and marred by insincerity as well. Surely there were better and more important things to say. Take it from a fellow-author who has been prevented by ill health from continuing in his profession, etc., etc. . . ."

Which of them to believe? If only I had twenty or thirty years more to live, I should end by reaping some advantage from all this disinterested advice, contradictory as so much of it is.

My object in quoting it is not to offend but to disclose by what methods a reader gets into touch with an author, to the point of fulfilling some imperative need. I believe there is no effective way of escaping his commandeering method. I also believe, after being thoroughly trained for nearly half a century to his arbitrary requirements, to the mad lack of restraint that guides the pens of lonely women, men with obsessions, and those monomaniacs who persist in asking questions, that I prefer their indiscretion to their silence.

" Madame,

" I send you my life's work; it consists of my impressions and opinions of the books I have read. I have left a blank page between the title and the text, and would ask you to be so kind as to write a preface on this. I shall call for the manuscript in a week's time. Believe me . . . etc., etc. . . .

" P.S. Please make the preface as long as possible."

May I never see God if I am lying, as we say where I come from! The weighty manuscript had been sent by registered post and at the cost of 146 francs to the sender.

" *Madame,*
" *I am thirteen and a half years old. All my life I have been obsessed by a craving to write. People have always told me that I have plenty of talent. But I have hesitated. And now I think it is too late to take such a serious step. My parents tell me that I must continue with my studies, but I have little interest in them. Would you oblige me, Madame, by giving me your opinion . . . etc., etc. . . .*"

The underlining of "all my life" and "always" is mine. As I read them I thought of the little boy-acrobat who rode his bicycle round and round the mosaic pavement at Chartres making dizzy figures of eight, with his hands off the handle-bars. I asked his bearded grandfather who was watching over him how old the child might be.

"Four and a half."

"Four and a half! And he rides like that!"

"Oh!" said the proud grand-parent, "he learnt when he was quite small."

I admire child gymnasts, but I am a little afraid of child writers. To start with, there are too many of them. Then who in the world would not be afraid of a child's vigour and ease of movement through the impenetrable? He lacks only the vocabulary to be our equal when the passion to write comes upon him. I could give the name, at any rate the pseudonym she has chosen to write under, of more than one girl of fifteen whose literary baggage already comprises a slim volume of poems, two plays, three if not more novels, and *Memoirs* (*sic*). There is the same facility among boys. Of course I feel no pressing hurry to form an opinion on so many youthful works, confided to me as they are without my consent. But I still retain my faculty for astonishment, even if it should only be for youthful writers' attempts to exploit their own novelty. Sometimes, it is true, they conceal their identity, but they never forget to state their age. "*Madame, I am thirteen, fourteen, fifteen years old . . .*" Do their parents, tutors and schoolteachers call them "little fiends, exclusively addicted to violent sports"? Certain it is that some of them are deceiving themselves, certain that some are being deceived. Certainly there is, in the almost child-like urgency and frankness of their efforts to reach us, something more than the mere itch to show off, something that comes very close to practice in perfecting the use of a weapon. "*Madame, I am so young!*" Almost I find in this a note which cannot be the cry of helplessness alone, and then I reproach myself for my suspicious nature. But the devil will out. "*Madame, do you not feel tempted to know how young I really am? Look at this . . .*" and out slips a photograph from the letter. What meaning should one attach to the sending of photographs—if a girl, hair in ringlets and the briefest of skirts; if a boy, in bathing-dress and the briefest of briefs? Well they know, these inspired children, that youth is always a weapon, and one deadlier than ever if it goes hand in hand with beauty.

Fate has decreed, where writing is concerned, that I should be incapable either of holding myself back or of giving instruction. What have I to teach, unless it be self-doubt, to those who since early youth have become secretly infatuated by self-love rather than by self-torture?

O you chorus of cynical child-writers. Children indeed you are, but what pain it is to know you cynical already, willing to sell yourselves to anyone who offers you leisure enough, bread enough, warmth enough, even solicitude enough—objects of barter all—just as it is difficult not to give you another thought! The whole problem seems solved for me when I hold to my vow never to listen to the echo which prolongs certain phrases: *"Madame, I am fifteen. All my life the imperative urge to write . . .".* From the brown paper parcel tied with string and containing sheets already crumpled and faded from having tried their luck elsewhere, there erupts, flutters, cascades—I cannot stop it—such an intoxicating odour of lies, heady despair, bumptious arrogance, craftily selected truth—an odour, did I say? No, a menace!

"It seems a pity to eat them," said Marcelle Blot.

"You're not compelled to, Marcelle."

All among my collection of paper-weights, tight-stuffed with curlicues, burnt sugar twists, flowers and small insects, Marcelle arranged her round, impeccably red tomatoes, with never a crease or a rib on them, the last tomatoes from her Saint-Cloud garden, and with a sigh murmured "Yes, it is compulsory. Because they are good."

There is about la Grande Marcelle, friend of artists—and my friend—a faint but pungent smell of tarragon,

chervil and parsley which she had arranged into a bunch
for me round a centrepiece of celery, white as ivory, and
sprigs of purple-flowering thyme. Whatever emerges
from her hands always has a suggestion of the skills of
weaver, braider, florist, and decorator. She dictates the
fashion in women's hats. And then, of a sudden, she
refuses to make any more hats. Because of the hats? No,
because of the women. She retires to Saint-Cloud, and
goes into retreat. She is so essentially unsociable! Yet it
was none other but she who invented the art of delicately
plaiting reeds and raffia into the shape of leaves and
making belts and sandals of them. I have seen her con-
trive a bridal wreath by imaginatively stringing white
pearls of mistletoe berries on the spikes of a branch of
thorns. She arrived from Saint-Cloud to pay me a visit,
graced with the tricolour of a healthy peasant woman,
blue eyes, white teeth, red cheeks.

"So you're not working at the moment, Marcelle?"

"Oh yes I am," she said. "I've constructed something
of such beauty that I waste all my time in admiring it. In
my garden I have four large privet bushes. I'm overrun
with privets, as it happens, and since I could see no future
for them as privet bushes, I wanted to be rid of them.
I've often wondered how they could best be improved,
and now I know. I hollowed out with the clippers the
entire centre of each clump, taking care to leave quite a
thick outer covering, and I removed every leaf from these
branches. Those I had snipped off I interwove in and
out of the ones I had left, till they made a basket, or
rather a cage—the sort of work I am good at—making
the most of a few little apertures here and there in the
close-knit weave. Through these I fitted transverse canes

across the inside, some to serve as perches and others on which to hang food and drink pans. Do you see the idea of my out-of-door cages? I have strengthened the weave on the side of the prevailing wind, and made it thicker still over the top, woven in the shape of a dome."

"And what do the birds say to that, Marcelle?"

She raised her hands in admiration. "The birds? They have talked so much about it that they've got practically nothing more to say. I'd hardly finished the first cage before they knew what it was for. If you could have heard the commotion among them! And their committee meetings, and the contradictory views expressed! I spend my time with them. I've seen three kinds of tit, bullfinches, chaffinches, and others I don't know the name of. My cat laughs behind his paw at me. He must be thinking I don't know the first thing about making a trap. The fact is . . ."

"But what about the birds themselves? Haven't they thought it might be a trap?"

Marcelle's azure blue eyes quizzed me for an instant. "No," she said. "They know who I am. They're already popping in and out through the small windows. The chaffinch goes in with its head down, cramped up like a parakeet. And just imagine, the others fly in and out at full tilt, the very opposite of birds who dislike being caged. It's overwhelming. They tell me that they'll be fighting for possession of my cages when spring comes round."

Marcelle thoughtfully closed down the lid of the basket in which she had brought me the latest adornments of her kitchen garden, before saying with a note of determination in her voice, "So much the worse, in that case. From now on I shall have to invent something to stop them fighting."

She tied her foulard under her chin and made to leave the room, but I called her back.

"Marcelle, Marcelle! Haven't you brought me back my little black velvet hat?"

She poked her beautiful rustic face round the half-open door.

"Did you ever! No, I have not! I've not had the time. My clients the privets were more pressed for time than you! For you hardly ever go out, and they sleep out of doors every night."

✐ IX *Grasse, 1948*

O<small>N</small> each successive day following the appearance of
the first fully ripened fig of the second crop, you can
count on any number up to a dozen "secondary figs"
being ripe and ready to fall into your hand, soft, with
inflexed necks, bearing the pheasant's eye mark at their
base and on their sides the parallel stripes that crackle
their tender skins of mauve and grey. For the first few
days you'll not be able to eat your fill. There's little to be
said for your appetite if you can't polish off six, ten, or
even a dozen figs with the chill of night still upon them;
they readily split apart and are as red inside as a
pomegranate. They are not as yet runny with their full
measure of honey-sweet stickiness, and are so much the
easier to put in the mouth.

But the figs multiply with the rapidly increasing rate
of maturity. Before the week is out the huge fig tree, the
young tree further down, and the contorted tree will all
be overwhelmed with ripe fruit, pendent from the neck
like the stocking nests of the Haitian cacique bird. There
is no end to them. Every single one deserves to be picked
and placed on a wicker tray. Time is of the essence, for
by now it is easy to see that in their turn the grapes are
insistent on being cut, that the tomatoes have reached the
peak of their red lacquer lavishness, and all that remain

on the peach trees are the fluffy little pellets destined to become the hard ammunition for children to pelt each other with.

After which the trees will bear no further crop but apples, in abundance down in the hollow of the valleys round Grasse and in the orchards of Solliés-Pont. Here and there one of the splendid expatriate Normandy pippins falls into the torrent bed of the Gapeau and bobs along to the astonishment of its now diminished stream.

I might very well have believed the factory for the slow processing of floral essences to be sound asleep within its extensive gardens, had not my arrival coincided with that of a dray drawn by a stout-limbed percheron and loaded with lengthy thick-wicker baskets, scrupulously veiled with heavy cloth. Nine hundred kilos of jasmine blossom were discharged from this rustic equipage. My wheel-chair became firmly stuck in their way.

Only four hours previously had they left the fields and they were still perfectly fresh. They were on their way to be consumed and they drew me along in their wake. An atmosphere that could have been cut with a knife existed beneath the ventilated ceilings, yet parted slowly before the silent footfall of the men employed in the service of perfume.

Nine hundred kilos of jasmine blossom lay in a still white litter where they had been summarily dumped on the polished flagstone floor, not far distant from another bed, of withering tube-roses that breathed out the odour of mortal decay yet still retained their flesh-coloured

pallor. From these inestimable stacks arose an aura of
consenting torpor, almost the desire to be quit of life;
there I willingly would have remained, physically, men-
tally, optimistically exhausted, under the watchful eye of
a young lady who had devoted her energies that morning
to pushing my wheel-chair. She was a delicious child and
I nicknamed her my little fairy horse. When I enquired in
some trepidation whether I were not too heavy, she tossed
her head up and down in a negative response: nothing
is too heavy for a little fairy horse.

The factory owner wished to guide me to the successive
fates that awaited in sealed vats the spoils garnered from
the various harvests of Grasse: no eye would ever look
upon them again as flowers.

The integrity of an industry such as his is an unrivalled
marvel. From jasmine is extracted the scent of jasmine,
and from iris bulbs the scent of iris. "If you were staying
a little longer at Grasse," Maurice Maubert said to me,
"I would show you the huge multicoloured mattresses of
freshly picked carnations that embalm the air with essence
of cloves."

When, on taking my leave of him, I asked at what stage
in the proceedings, by what stress of cunning, the scent
of jasmine reappeared in the extract of jasmine, he slipped
into my hands a packet of that compound known as "*le
concret*", resembling a cake of dark, sticky chocolate,
thanks to which, though I had barely touched it, I not
long after established the fact that boiled eggs smell of
jasmine, that fish salad tastes of jasmine, that baked aubergine and crème caramel follow suit. The man responsible for such an excess of perfumed delights offered no
excuse for it, quite the contrary: he filled my cup with

hot coffee vaguely enraptured by jasmine, saying "What
better proof could I have given you that this concentrated
essence of jasmine is irrepressible? "

Toward six in the evening the scent of jasmine begins
to bar the roads as effectively as a rope stretched taut
across them. All night long and until first light the
flowers will make their invisible presence increasingly
potent. All the same, as we pass by on nights the blue of
wood ash in the moon's absence we can distinguish the
little starry blossoms, white against the dark foliage.
Between dawn and sunrise there is time enough for a
picking, with nimble fingers that pluck only the corollas
and leave behind the tiny sepals. The jasmine bushes are
trussed into loose sheaves, both to facilitate the picking
and to prevent the flowers from coming into contact with
the light soil in which tuberose and sweet onions flourish
side by side, and also to spare them the weight of so much
as an ant, a grain of sand, or a ladybird!
On evenings when a heat haze reminds us that August
is nearing its end, my crippled condition earns me a run
in the car. The region round Grasse—which has no summer rainfall—secretes a wealth of subterranean streams.
Gushing springs abound, the smallest *mas* has its miniature cascade; each village is supplied with a constant flow
of water from the three all but ice-cold jets of a full-bodied
stone urn in the *placette*, and often enough this water is
beaded with tiny bubbles; at all costs I have to borrow a
cup, or drink from the pitcher attached to the fountain-
head, as I was wont to do in the past when travelling
through Aix-en-Provence. A spring is an eternal miracle.

A property up for sale, where the carriage ways are open to certain visitors, is a babble of bubbling brooks, a simmering of freshets in the shade; with a flourish of crystalline muscles, a solid arm of water gushes up from a gash in the ground. On the tenantless terrace, in the area surrounding a single-pedestalled fountain, time, moisture, birds and winged seeds between them have contributed to the formation of a vast vegetal sponge, where each blade sheds its pearly tear, as at the ancient fountain at Salon.

Whether they break surface or remain beneath it, the waters of Grasse, in the unbroken silence of the pure night air, create an elusive mist in which the jasmine fragrance is entangled and held captive. Nothing stirs before the peep of dawn. As the last stars fade from the heavens and a reddish brown bar rises along the horizon, we are but three—my dearest friend, a striped cat and myself—who infringe the laws of sleep, perched on the heights above the gradation of cultivated terraces. Before ten in the morning there will not be a breath of air to ruffle the leaves of the crinkled, misshapen mulberry, or those of the young plane trees. It was the same at Saint-Tropez, where we used to wait under the huddled wistaria for the moment when the wind from the west and the sun, in conjugation, awoke the sea, the cicadas, the morning glory, and the purslane of four differing colours. In those days, with the confidence of my fifty years, I would stir the sleeping waters to frighten the shy reptilia by dipping my foot in the pools, pick the mauve statice in the salty marsh and at that incomparable hour I would be saddened by the thought that after the first bathe I should have to retire within my shuttered house

and work at *Break of Day*. I no longer possess that
house, and it is a far hark back to my fiftieth birthday.
What is left to me is my avidity. Of all my forces it alone
has not humbled itself to time.

I am shown none but the most beautiful things. The
kind attentions of my friends, never entirely devoid of
humour, ensure that I am taken out for a drive of fifteen
miles or so along the whole length of the Croisette, at the
very time when among the concourse of bathers the nude
figures of a man and a woman are on the point of
clambering out of the water on to a float, at the precise
moment when one man among a host of others in search
of refreshment is staking his claim for a place at the
pedestal table for himself and his fruit juice, where one
bare back may be heard saying to the bare back beside it
in a tone of defiance " But I tell you I've gone a far darker
colour than you ". I find the spectacle so strange that I
insist, as at a merry-go-round, on having another turn.
    Out at sea a boat is towing its pair of water-skis, for all
the world like a silvery insect at the end of a line. In their
coupled state, and lent enchantment by the distance, their
pairing is the only one down here that evokes the idea of
love. As for the rest . . . I do not believe I have ever
seen a crowd less concerned with love, or so stripped to
the buff, as this Cannes Vintage of 1948. They look just
about as voluptuous as a keg of sardines, packed in their
serried ranks. Let it be said, however, that here the
weather is fine, whereas everywhere else it is raining.
" Just one turn more? " I am granted it, driving along
at a snail's pace between the sea and the dressmakers', the

sea and the jewellers', the sea and the sandal-sellers, the
vendors of brassières and fruit juices, the sea and hotels,
cars, flowerstalls, sun-bathers and walnut-stained women.
One yellow hotel has exceeded all reasonable proportions,
making a mock of architectural harmony. An orchestra
strives to make its feeble strains audible in the open air.
I observe women who, in the guise of bathing costumes,
wear creased or uncreased shorts of poor quality flowered
fabrics and gorgerins like the hollows of one's hands.
Such is their promenading attire of an afternoon; the hem
above the thighs greasy and dirtied by oil. The men, in
the security of a brief and highly revealing slip, give a
far better account of themselves. No matter, there are
far too many of them, men and women alike. " Would
you care to take another turn? "—" No thanks! " I find it
hard to tell whether all this varied display of human
flesh is turning me into a vegetarian, or whether I am
shockingly jealous of those who apparently derive pleasure
from their own agility, the briny, and going naked. I
go back gladly to the slopes of Grasse, though this means
that I must be parted from the sea. It lies beyond the line
of little hills—over there, look!—between those two little
breasts rising from this land that breathes so easily. It's
not so very far away; you'd almost think that by standing
on tiptoe . . . Let us resign ourselves: the sea is not
visible from here. You won't console me by referring
jokingly to the Mediterranean as being hardly worth
calling a sea. There is little doubt, when the mood is on
it, this sea knows only too well how to bring havoc to the
Côte d'Azur.

When at Hyères, though from quite a distance, we
could see its hard lapis blue and its wind-rows of sand.

From where we are now I am taken sometimes in the morning to La Garoupe and dumped down there on the wave-splashed spit of the shore. Below the balustrade the foaming sea joins in the frolics of the naked children; to my now useless feet the feel of the sand is sometimes cool, sometimes warm. At Antibes the evening before last, all along the sea-wall where I was being promenaded in my chair, I saw the sea far better for it being a moonlit night, and for the fact that my turning-point happened to be at the spot where a restaurateur of genius, by placing his tables exactly in the centre of the arc formed by the rampart, has provided his summer clients with an ideal view. On one side are the port and quayside, on the other, in due course and when their hour has struck, appear the light of the moon, the flares of the fishing smacks, and the phosphorescent back of a breaking wave. That night we all felt that nothing could go wrong and everything we could wish for was ours. The patron, brown as a berry and dressed in white tight-fitting clothes from collar to espadrilles, was wreathed in smiles as he came and went with silent tread, chatting freely in anticipation of a long July night devoted to good food and drink.

Between our tables in the foreground and the distant backcloth there passed, some stopping and others not, a succession of those disconcerting touring cars that are to be seen eating up the miles on all roads, noiseless as often as not, yet whose very discretion renders them the more dangerous since, gleaming from the final authoritative flick of the polisher, they seem to rise from an oil-bath only to plunge back into it the very next moment.

The white-clad proprieter felt no apprehension as he watched them approach. He had the knack of applying an

American, Venezuelan, Scandinavian, or Swiss name to every dress and every face behind its tanned mask that drew up in front of his premises. Sure of himself, certain of his minions keenly employed in cooking and gossiping in the recesses of his kingdom, he would disappear only to reappear in a twinkling, arms laden, to set before his guests from Chile or Colombia a long dish of raw vegetables, white fish piled high, a firm-fleshed *rascasse*, and, the pride of the evening, a luscious langouste ready dressed in its rose red carapace.

Few and far between, along the Côte, are the wayside inns constrained—like the chronometer at Marseilles which struck the hour for you every forty-five minutes— to 'fit' their season into two-and-a-half months and to keep alive their fame and fortune within that limit of time. The finical tourist—certain of that ilk do still exist —known to the natives of Provence as *l'estrangier,* can tot them up on the fingers of one hand. He makes a bee-line for them, and emerges properly stung. Yet he returns to them again and again. He is a devotee of the mysteries of the French cuisine, for all that he may well ruin his palate by preliminary libations of alcohol. I watched him at work the other evening in one of those enchanting spots to be found in the Midi where everything in the garden is lovely: trees properly tended, plants and shrubs well watered, maidservants with plump rounded arms which, the Lord be praised, are kept too busy ever to grow thin, where mint and basil vie with lemon-scented verbena in an atmosphere already fragrant with rose-geranium, suggestive of Morocco.

By half past nine, my four table-companions and I were feeling pleasantly replete after dining off small red-fleshed melons, white-fleshed fish, *courges gratinées*, peaches, our glasses still holding the glint of a young wine—how difficult nowadays to come by this *tendron du pays!*— when our eyes were arrested by the arrival of the invaders, people who never think of dining before ten and who must have a drink before they eat.

It was up to the hard-working staff to satisfy their every whim. Into the hands of each was put an identical, heavily moulded glass embossed with tortuous scrolls, over which passed a multicoloured cloud-burst of pastis, cocktails, and champagne. In a twinkling the bright fire of the drinks was dimmed by the clink of cubic bonbons of ice.

Showing a certain reluctance to be seated, one or two clinging couples remained on their feet and began to go through the vague motions of a dance. Yelping females intrigued in particular for the embrace of an American film-star, a man of dubious age, long since gone to seed and slap-happy in his cups.

Another time, and in another place, I came to a halt beside an inn that lay just off a main road and sparkled like an elongated island edged with lights and flowers behind its fringe of parked cars. Enthroned in state at the entrance sat she whose presence ensured the prosperity of the house, *la patronne,* its organiser and its guarantor. Vast in bulk, she made no bones about it, knowing full well that in her noble and strenuous calling there is no authority without fulness of figure. Her impartial smile provoked no jealousies, yet behind it lurked a hint of irony. Her speech was concise, clipped, with a detectable disdain: her " Fish? Meat? Both? ", a typical example. " What have you got in the way of meat? " asked an impertinent fellow, assuming, as he hoped, something of the air of an habitué. Sizing him up, she administered a single word snub: "All." The whipper-snapper, disappointed, shifted his ground. "I'd rather have fish. What fish have you got? " "All," the good lady repeated. How my heart warmed to her, how infinitely superior she was to the man who was trying to find something "difficult" on her menu! He chose *truite au bleu* followed by a *ris de veau*. The lady of the house, merciful after her fashion, saw to it that a touch of authentic thick cream was added to the sauce of the sweetbreads. Not but what, the meddlesome diner was not deterred from taking a squint to his right at my piping hot, velvety fish soup, and to his left at a fourfold crêpe, oozing with a bubbly cheese fondant, a speciality of the house.

There is a time and a place for everything. Here we are not assailed by any such twinge of conscience as, in Paris, may reduce us to reprobates when faced by a display of exorbitantly priced delicacies, for here we are proffered in profusion, by hands rich in cunning and traditional skills, the fruits, fish and game of Provence, brought in direct from the kitchen garden or still alive from the farmyard, landed from the sea or from fresh water tanks, or even poached from the neighbouring pine tracts. Heavens! how readily we revert to a state of savage euphoria, eager to set off in pursuit of the black pig in the forests of Tahiti as to sample that imaginary dish which in my part of the country both symbolises and ridicules the extreme of luxury, the dish known as *"fersues de caquesiau"*, or, in plain words, "midges' livers". We fly from one extreme to the other: either the shell-fish bristling with legs and claws and coral-trimmings, or else a snack by the road side, a *casse croute marseillais*, soaked in good oil and garlic.

We have only to transplant ourselves, by a turn of the wheel over the dial of France, and we are no longer recognisable, so easily do we become amenable to nature's bounty. Beneath the fig-tree, under the sky-blue plumbago, let yourself go and take your ease in the midst of pimento, sea-urchin, and a well-stocked salad-bowl, with *loup-de-mer* at a thousand francs each and out-of-season game *sur canapé*, let yourself go, openly and in the sight of all! Nothing that we enjoy eating need cause us shame. Nothing is too beautiful or too good to put the finishing touch—just once in a while, what say you?—to the natural lavishness that surrounds us, even though we have to be ready to renounce it all once the time comes for returning to the long, dietary discomfort that has for so long been our portion for three out of the four seasons.

There is always the return journey to be made. We have to leave that which we love and deserves our love, that which touches our heart no less than that which makes us laugh, as for instance the basset hound who could work up an appetite only to the sound and fury of his own pretended ferociousness; no longer can we look forward to a pattering of feet and a morning visit, no longer listen to the prattle of the diminutive artiste who, at the age of eight, displayed both on stage and screen the skill and aplomb of an old stager.

The troublesome question of my return to Paris became the subject of a friendly discussion in my presence. " No, not by train. Anything rather than the train for her. The

heat! The car's out of the question.—Why so?—Takes
too long. Not comfortable enough.—Right. Then it
means by air.—Oh, I don't much like the thought of her
going by air . . . —But what, after all, would she like
best?—She's not said anything."

She's not said a word. She's not heard, she was reading. She was trying not to laugh. My dearest friend
glanced in my direction—what had I got to say? He
weighed me up. How best pack an object that one
moment agrees to everything, and the next reacts in the
strongest possible terms! Where can a basket be found
to take this great cat on a journey a thousand miles long?
But the cat made up its own mind, and the object gave
herself the pleasure of cutting short the debate and
choosing to go by air. It is pleasant on occasion to assume
the prerogative of a foreman of the jury and decide the
issue by a casting vote.

My wheel-chair out on the tarmac, then the hot air
bath while waiting for the take-off, the frail of newspapers, a pinch of absorbent cotton-wool to caulk the ears,
the neat little lunch-basket and the flagon of wine, all of
them prime necessities when travelling Air-France, for
I become bored in a plane. Nothing up there is to my
liking except the speed. "See, we still have a strip of the
sea to cross! Do look, that ribbon of a road down there,
surely that's the very route we took last week!" A fig
for the route, and for the unexpected cloud we pierce
straight through as though it were a cocoon!

I confess my inaptitude. Once before, on the Toulouse-
Fez-Toulouse circuit, I realised that riding on high is not
for me. My flights of fancy do not rise above ground level.
"Look down there, do you know that we are passing

right over your native heath? " And do you believe, companion mine, that I am going to recognise my native heath in this flying mist with its criss-crossing roads, its chequerboard of fields cloven by a streak of water you tell me is the Yonne? Not a hope! One thing is certain. Even if I do happen to draw my inspiration from the malicious sense of fun that lies at the ever impenitent heart of septuagenarians, even if I do have to reckon with my impotence and at the same time with the spirit of curiosity engendered by it, I never wish to travel by air again unless it is a question of saving precious hours. Whilst I am being borne along by it I forget the aircraft, for it possesses the magic power of eliminating distances. Thus all we have contact with is the point of departure and the distant goal which looms up out of nowhere before our eyes. My flights of fancy remain on ground level. But you, winged monster, you withhold them from me, for you alone can make the descent! It is the descent and not the sudden uprush into the wilderness of clouds that I find enchanting. Four hours, it takes you but four hours to muster a miniature France beneath your wings, crushing her mountains, obliterating her towns. Finally I achieve the greatest miracle of all: my red and white room, the bed on which I navigate my own course, the stage moonlight of my blue lantern: all that, and I did not know it, is but four hours from Nice.

Our first meeting—1894 or '95?—took place before lunch at the house of Catulle Mendès. The sun was streaming into the room and at that mid-day hour its light gave a vivid outline to the long silhouetted figure of a slight young woman who was leaning forward under the weight of the load she was carrying; this turned out to be a fine, heavy child of between eighteen months and two years old. Fair as summer, he turned to look at me with his grave dark eyes, inherited from his mother.

This splendid child, whose birth had all but caused the death of so frail a mother, this child of light himself died of meningitis before he was three, after battling against death with a strength already far beyond his years. There are few of us left now who remember his short life. And I believe that Moreno—the lovely, austere name chosen by Marguerite Moreno—hardly ever spoke of him except to those of her own age who, like myself, had caught a glimpse of this son of too early promise during his brief existence.

In the home of Catulle Mendès I failed to pay proper attention either to the excellent coffee prepared with his own hands, or to the anti-Semitic couplet, always to hand, which enhanced his reputation as a wit. I had neither eyes nor ears for anything but the tall young woman.

Her own wit, the easy and sparkling delivery of her words, the timbre of her voice which rejoiced the ear of the listener, the unredeemed pallor of her complexion, a head of magnificent chestnut hair with here and there a glint of gold! I can still see the warm look in her unwavering, lively eyes that scorned any coquettish appeal. Everything about her humiliated and enchanted the exiled country lass that I was at the time. From the first moment of this encounter I admired and adored Marguerite Moreno. The astonishing thing is that she returned my affection. We were young enough, having both recently come of age, for our friendship to develop into the sort of schoolgirl crush which young ladies at boarding schools find so intoxicating. Throughout the period that Mendès contributed theatrical notices to *Le Journal*, he would frequently take us both to the critic's box. I squeezed myself in between his crumpled shirt-front and Moreno's lovely swanlike neck. One night he took us to a music hall.

"You're going to see the strangest little creature," Marguerite said to me. "Any producer worth his salt ought to grab hold of her and rescue her from herself and her idiotic songs. Even from her stage-name, which is quite ridiculous. She's gifted with the most attractive ugliness, and she looks as if she invented her own dance numbers."

At that time Polaire was twirling and spinning on the boards of the Scala, like a midge caught in a sunbeam. She had not yet had her auburn hair cut short—auburn, mind you, not black. Her stage costume, the perfectly cut dress of a period "smasher", did credit to the taste and talent of Madame Landolff who, as a costumière, has had no equal. A full, short, nondescript skirt concealed, when not in motion, its embroidered underside ablaze with concentric circles of all the colours of a rainbow. The least twitch made by the midget singer—during the reprise she danced with eyes shut and arms stiff like a woman falling asleep—would unfurl about her, around legs in a froth of black lace, the seven reverberant colours. Her hair, swept up and back and twisted into a clown's topknot, displayed two exquisite ears, which later in her career were hidden by her short hairstyle.

Madame Landolff delighted in designing dresses for her, all of which seemed deserving of a better fate than a music-hall turn. I well remember one of white lace, like rigid spindrift against that brown statuette. I can see another, a miracle of rustling silk resembling paper, in dark and ever-changing shades of green, slashed with a hundred small cuts that opened upon an acid pink foundation during the dance; a mat terra cotta dress closely matching her skin, which appeared to be naked, decked with a few mauve feathers.

" What did I tell you? " said Moreno. " She looks like nobody else. Perhaps she is a wraith after all."

For at that time Moreno herself was unaware whose compelling hand it was that would drag the dancing and singing, rainbow-encircled Polaire away to the legitimate theatre.

I am forever losing only to discover afresh my very earliest memories of Marguerite Moreno, for the lives we both led tended to scatter and then reassemble them. She travelled far and wide, I never stirred. We both got married, became unmarried, married again. She dwelt in the pure regions of poetry, and tried her hand at imparting higher education to the Argentians; I played in pantomime at the Apollo and elsewhere. After lengthy silences, which caused me to fear the worst, an exchange of letters would put us back where we were, at the heart of an unbroken friendship. On leaving the Argentine, she returned to the stage in one of those deplorable plays by Bataille that were saved only by their cast—Bady, Yvonne de Bray, Huguenet.

She staged her return at the Vaudeville, in *La Phalène*.

During my pregnancy I used to hoist my burdened body up to her dressing-room where, of an evening, she would lavish on me in short flashes the colour, flavour, adventures and disillusionments of her sojourn in the Argentine. "Yes, yes, *mon vieux*, the very first night, a butterfly the size of a vulture, with a luminous nose, flapped all over my room making as much din as a threshing-machine! Didn't you hear my cries for help from here? " She knew how highly I prized a description depicted in the strongest colours, the delight I took in the enlargement of the thing described, and we would " mon vieux " each other like children at a village school.

Today I find it surprising that at the very time when she attained the full glory of womanhood, when thanks to the Argentinian climate she returned with healthier cheeks and a fuller bust (in the title rôle of *The Green God* she showed off her superb long legs), she should have dropped her charming and romantic first name. Her public called her "Moreno". Her friends and ardent admirers—she always had them in abundance—referred to her as "Moreno", a dusky name that beautifully suited her matchless pallor with its suggestive hidalgo look. When she was acclaimed a star celebrity, when the

vast array of cinema-goers became infatuated with her
trenchant yet restrained gift for playing comedy, as a
delicate act of gratitude the crowds restored to her her
lovely christian name. In all public places it was hurled
at her. "Marguerite . . . there's Marguerite!" More
intimidated than she wished to let it appear, she would
flutter her eyelashes when struck by this flower.

After Marcel Schwob, who was madly in love with her,
she was married for a time to Jean Daragon, the actor, on
whom a false beard could confer the elegant virility of
The Ironmaster by Georges Ohnet, or the poetic hirsute-
ness of Richepin's *The Tramp*. Ill health kept Daragon
out of the First War, and no woman ever excelled Moreno
in lightening the protective yoke as she watched over this
man of fragile health camouflaged as a bruiser in the
pink of condition. So skilful was her gentle raillery that
he never detected the anxiety or the pity behind her
smiling mask. But she was unable to prevent him from
dying even though she took him with her to Nice, where
she worked in a hospital for the wounded. If only I had
kept every one of the letters she wrote to me at that
time!

"I carry on with my duties among my legless ones, who
are gay, and my armless ones, who are sad. It doesn't take
long before my legless ones are drawing, writing, making
small toys, propelling themselves from place to place as
best they can, and getting up to every sort of nonsense.
Whereas my armless ones grow melancholy: because for
a man it must be the greatest humiliation, perhaps the
worst of all, never again to be able to undo his own
trouser buttons without a helping hand."

For long months of the long war we both remained

faithful to Paris, living as near neighbours. She lived on the ground floor of a modern house in Rue Jean-de-Bologne and I in a Swiss chalet in Rue Cortambert. Annie de Pène had a cottage, with steps running up to it, at the very end of the countrified Herrent blind-alley. Musidora had recently done up one of those bachelor establishments, in a wedge-shaped gore in Rue Decamps, a single room, with hot water, central heating, and bathroom "with every convenience", that put to shame anything our tottering houses in old Passy had to offer. On nights when the sky was peopled with Zeppelins, she would sleep at Rue Cortambert on a small iron bed, and do the shopping and cooking in the day time. I acted as char and did the washing. We made up a fine female squad! We used to tie the hand-washed sheets round a stout copper faucet and wring them out by twisting them tight, while Marguerite Moreno, a cigarette between her lips, would sprinkle our domestic chores with the beneficent dew of news, true or false, anecdotes, and prognostications. Annie de Pène knew of a certain carriage gateway beneath which a man from the country sold chickens, tossing them over to her with an "Up she goes, little lady! Now chuck me my four francs five sous!"

It was the hardest thing in the world for us to break up for the night. From those black times dates Moreno's inspiring influence on Annie de Pène, on her daughter Germaine Beaumont, and on Musidora. We drank in the consolation of lovely words, sinuous verse, the distant scene, all magically evoked. In the shadow of Moreno followed Jean Daragon, bulky and breathing with difficulty. My little garden brought forth its usual offerings and, after a watering, exhaled its garden smells. My daughter was enjoying life in the unravaged Limousin; the finest Paris peaches cost five sous apiece.

All the members of our phalanstery of the XVIth arrondissement owed a debt of gratitude to Moreno, for there she sowed the good seed of laughter, inimitably, miraculously, the laughter of crises, the nervous, unrestrained laughter of war-time, self-assertive insolence in face of looming danger, the cut and thrust of wordplay as intoxicating as drafts of wine. On windless nights the belch of the howitzers, each distinct, reached us from the east. This deep-seated, close-sounding concussion had the effect of silencing conversation, and was transmitted through the distorted regions of the air to reach as far as our deserted but keenly alert quarters. It happened one night that Moreno, doubtless at a loss for verbal quips, became engrossed in the rhythm of the cannonade, snapping her fingers and clicking her heels as it rose and fell, and improvising on the spot a mock-Spanish dance; with a twist of her hips and a roll of her eyes she restored laughter to our midst, banishing all thought of danger by a display of healthy impertinence with the temerity of a heroine. Pierre Fresnay can surely not have forgotten a post-war occasion at Marseilles, when we, Marguerite, he and I, were leaving the theatre about midnight after playing in *Chéri!* Moreno was brilliant in her improvisations as she sniffed the aniseed-laden air of the Cannebière and instructed Fresnay in the joyous adventures of nomadic life. She left him doubled up with laughter, completely dazzled by her arresting glance and the wide range of her fanciful imagination.

I can still see the gasping tip of her cigarette that was hardly ever stubbed out—"Marguerite, you're smoking

too much "—her honest appetite that never boggled at
the foie gras and black pudding of the snack-bars—
"Marguerite, you'll make yourself ill! " Her own special
gifts, and among them I would choose the sudden serious-
ness and fullest over-tone accorded to the measure of the
alexandrine, and the healing magic to charm all creatures,
for I benefited from them for more than fifty years, but
intermittently, alas! One cannot always have the good
fortune to play Léa in *Chéri* when Madame Moreno has
consented to play the part of Charlotte Peloux! In
Brussels, as elsewhere, I learned many a lesson from her
genuinely roving accomplishments. She would watch me
with detachment as I arranged a writing-table, put three
flowers into a vase, or set out on a plate a bunch of fresh
but insipid large grapes. Already up in her room she had
half-unpacked her valise, hung up her scotch cape, and
chucked a packet of cigarettes and the day's paper on the
table. On going into it I would exclaim "Marguerite
Moreno's room, I can tell by the smell of it." For a linger-
ing personal fragrance, to which my keen sense of smell
has always been highly susceptible, denoted her presence.
Nothing whatever to do with body odour, it was not
axillary—"I'm drier than tinder," she was in the habit
of saying—nor did it derive from any perfumed essence
or lotion.

The particular place on her neck below the ear, where
I would give her a kiss of greeting, was embalmed with
the invariable, captivating scent of her skin, as well as
that of tobacco smoke. All you many men who have at
some time or other been violently in love with Marguerite,
you at least can never have failed to note, never have

forgotten the scent exhaled by her glorious, creamy skin, with a hint of amber beneath its white texture!

An hotel bedroom, by no means the best, a valise or two, a book, two volumes of verse, a manuscript, a cape, *the* cape—a reversible tartan—that she would lend to anyone in need of it (it once saved my dearest friend and me from a downpour of hail that lashed our open carriage), from this meagre assortment of props she was capable of creating comic effects by sheer force of will. On the stage, a gold or silver shoe might occasionally peep out from beneath the hem of her skirt; the foot it shod, worthy of the fairest raiment and itself beyond compare, was designed for freedom and, naked, to tread the coolness of flagstones, a foot such as that of M'Barka, the bare-foot dancing-girl of the Pasha of Marrakesh.

When touring the provinces Moreno and I were sometimes able to keep together. Pierre Moreno used to play Patron, the boxing instructor, in *Chéri*. Every now and again he would work off his homesickness by singing songs in his native Gascon dialect, well suited to his delightful tenor voice. All three of us loved Brussels, the gilt of its Grande Place, the busy gaiety of its inhabitants, the beer, the coffee, the buttered slices of tasty Belgian bread; while sitting outside that huge restaurant, you must know it, *Les Trois* . . . whatever it was, we would bathe in the stream of passers-by and enjoy our bohemian idleness to the full.

Moreno did not put aside much money from her earnings at that time. Later on the cinema woke up to the fact that it was worth their while to offer her a fortune. She accepted with disillusioned serenity. She owned certain properties, among them an exceptionally blue " Blue

Spring ", an ancient castle, as well as patrimony and land more than sufficient to satisfy her needs. Who could have imagined that the first few months of 1948 would be the last of her life! According to the demands made on her by cinema, theatre, and late-night cabaret, she pitched her tent first in an hotel in the Batignolles district before moving to one in the Avenue de l'Opéra. Knowing that I had for some time been unable to stir from my room, she would conquer any feelings of fatigue, walk a little way along the Avenue de l'Opéra, take for fun one of the little passages that honeycomb the Palais Royal, climb up the flight and a half to where I lay, and appear decked out in her usual array; cigarette, felt hat pulled down over one eye, and coat the colour of dusk and rain. Oh, how grateful I was to her for being always her own true self, ready to set off again and again, fagged out but untiring! How I loved her perpetual motion which, truth to tell, never parted me from her, loved her for her regularity in writing to me when far away, her zest for work which seemed to keep her young! I would make the pretence of putting her through a severe cross-examination.

"Marguerite, I demand nothing but the truth. Where have you come from? "

"From Courbevoie. I'm filming."

"What is the film? "

"Less than nothing, as you might suppose. And I had a matinée at the A.B.C."

"Are you hungry? Thirsty? "

"I had lunch in the taxi. But rest assured, tonight I'll have a bite of foie gras and champagne. Always supposing I have the time. You see, I have two performances at the A.B.C. and I've promised to go back to Courbevoie."

"When?"

"In . . . in ten minutes. After that, as you know, I'm giving a poetry reading at Tonton's at midnight."

"How many more nights have you got to put in at Tonton's?"

Her lovely hand flew to my shoulder and, with a gentle look, she stared me straight in the face.

"That, Macolette, is something I never wish to come to an end! Cabaret, as I have come to know, is something unique. Just think of it, I'm in the process of teaching them Verlaine. *They* gulped down Baudelaire like an untried drink. If only you could see them! For the most part, they have come there for the champagne, and the hell of it. I wrung their withers with Hugo and Delavigne all right, that was relatively easy work. But to lead them to the water of Baudelaire and Verlaine! With the slightest encouragement I'll win them over to Mallarmé! There I sit surrounded by their heat and their smell, their knees make room—but not always—for mine, by making a long arm I get a light off one of them, I fish for a cigarette in the cases held out to me. You can picture the scene! You hear them bawling, then watch them gradually grow silent till you feel they are listening. It's like the courts of heaven, with the crowd pressing in upon the speaker."

She lowered her eyes with pride, showing a reserve in which I have many a time found, a purely personal discovery, a look approaching sensuality. Now that she will never again stand beside the divan-bed, never again be the life and soul of Tonton's overheated cabaret, why should I conceal from my reader one trait among a hundred others in my attempted portrait of Marguerite? This lowering of the eyelids, which was her way of breaking in on a phrase, of hiding a part of her thought, was one of the rare movements, lasting but a moment, that to my mind brought to Moreno's broad, austere, pale features a significant flash of sensual pleasure.

After giving a defiant laugh, and making me laugh with her, she asked what time it was, hurriedly drew her coat round her, hurriedly made for the door after bending her tall figure over my raft that I might kiss Marguerite's fragrance, under her ear. But she remembered before leaving the room to point on her own body to the seat of some discomfiture "Bitch of a leg, and now this sciatica!"

Perhaps her object was to prevent me in my half-helpless state from envying her lovely slender feet, still capable of going up and down the staircase of the Palais Royal unaided.

She liked to see me alone, when no one else was there. She liked to see Madame Brisson alone, or one or other of her daughters. She liked to see Jeanne Roze without me, and Pierre Blanchar when no third person was present. More than I could name, and I don't believe I knew them all, were those with whom Marguerite Moreno loved to hobnob tête-à-tête. All of us, without exception, showed ourselves jealous of the moments that she spared for each one of us. What we had to have was Marguerite Moreno between our window and our fireplace, the famous felt hat, for so it became, pulled down over one eye, her well-worn vanity bag, her cigarettes, her untiring voice. I was sorry when she gave up wearing

her hair in the style that became so long the hallmark of
every rôle she played, the neat well-groomed cut of a man-
about-town, exactly fitting the shape of her head. At her
wrist jangled a wide-linked gold bracelet. What more can
I recollect of her who showed contempt for all outward
finery? A ring? Probably. But one's eye rested not on the
ring but on the hand, a hand needlessly elongated and
exaggerated in its refinement in the portrait that now
hangs in the Luxembourg. I can forgive the artist,
Granier, in favour of the speaking likeness; there, at its
frankest, with every dissembled thought removed, there
is the face of Marguerite Moreno between the age of
twenty and twenty-five.

She suffered considerably, I believe, and with barely
a word of complaint, from the life of the film-studios.
It is a cruel life for sensitive minds and bodies, in that it
brings face to face beings who were particularly intended
never to confront one another—a form of brutality from
which life in the wings of a theatre has been up till now
exempt. During the hours in the studio when she was not
on the set, Marguerite, respected by all, withdrew herself
to the best of her ability behind a screen of newspapers,
feigning drowsiness or a desire for rest. Her perfect manners, which made it impossible for her to snub or show
the least sign of impatience, did not come to her effort-
lessly, I am convinced. Many were the times when I tried
to question her about those working days which began
at dawn in an outer suburb, the endless rehearsals during
which the player extracts from the part, like pus from a
gathering, some short phrase that has to be tested for
sound over and over again, until its sterling worth is
proved by its ring and practice has made it indiscernibly

perfect. I still remain wilfully ignorant of the silver screen and its various techniques, a fact that proves me a person not only of a certain age but, as they say, of another age altogether.

Marguerite would tell me little or nothing in reply; shaking her head, she would gently say "You simply cannot imagine what the life of a film actor or actress is like. Impossible, I tell you. I have accepted it, I have no cause either for reproach or explanation. Macolette, drop the subject."

I have already spoken of her various abodes, of her gift for imposing her personality on them however commonplace they were to start with. It would seem that pure chance guided her choice. Rue Jean-de-Bologne, Rue Saint-Louis-en-l'Ile, Rue Notre-Dame-des-Champs, Boulevard du Montparnasse. But the moment she was in them, they became worthy of her presence. Whether she really cared for them I cannot be sure, it was I who became attached to them. Never shall I forget her kindness to me when she was lodging in Place Pereire, at a time when I stood in great need of moral support and could go for it to none but Marguerite. I would climb her stairs and ring the bell at the half-landing. In her room I remember a rough Spanish chest, a round table, the single place laid on it encroached on by a number of books, the books themselves forced into retreat by a strong cheese, a foie gras or some form of sausage meat, all from the Lot. The sun entered from the right quarter. The plum tart came from the near-by confectioner's. "Help yourself, Macolette.—I'm not hungry.—If you're feeling peckish, help yourself. Food is good for you in the state you're in. Sit down. I'm going to tell you the story of my life and of my miracles."

I wonder who is the present tenant of that low-ceilinged lodging from which has departed, if not the sunbeam, at least the presence that bestowed on it meaning and life! Marguerite Moreno left it as she left all the others, neither on sudden impulse nor from dislike. She particularly liked, I think, her last Paris domicile—I do not count hotels—Boulevard du Montparnasse, within easy distance of the blazing Rotonde, the warm glow of the many-coloured brasseries, the combination of deference and familiarity that escorted and vociferously saluted Marguerite Moreno along the wide sidewalks of the avenue.

Previously she had frequented the grey cement of some sort of new-style barracks, and about 1900—with Marcel Schwob—the period wood-panelling and frigid elegance of a house on the Ile Saint-Louis. The creamy white and narrow bourgeois respectability of Rue d'Argenteuil held no terrors for her. A few months before the end she was cracking up to me the genial good-nature and coun-trified fun of a family pension near the Batignolles. She also cracked them up to Pierre Moreno, who began to worry, came up to town from Touzac and found her in one of those hotels whose secret belongs to Paris and which are never without an antimacassared drawing room or a large, lavishly dismal garden. By dint of per-suasion and authority he succeeded in winning her away from this romantic background and establishing her in more up-to-date comfort. But she complained about it to me and, despite all Pierre Moreno's solicitude, her kindly hosts were not prevented from shedding copious and heart-felt tears at her departure. " I should have liked

to stay on there a little longer to please them," she confided to me. "They were so nice." How I adored the
occasional weakness of one who gave every outward
appearance of being able to measure up to both the
dangers of living alone and those of a life *à deux* with the
same unwavering eye.

I had the pleasure of applauding Moreno in *La Folle
de Chaillot*. A sharp attack of arthritis made me fear up
to the last moment that I should have to stay at home. But
I was sustained by the good wishes of my friends and
overcame my reluctance. Jouvet gave me his stage box,
my dearest friend his arm, and a lady unknown to me her
unexpected and providential shoulder, at the very moment
when I was about to collapse in the foyer. I attached considerable importance to that evening performance. Before
long Paris was to show even more regard and enthusiasm
than myself. I found at the Athénée exactly what I had
anticipated: virtuosity in the acting, Giraudoux in an
ebullient mood, and in myself a certain lack of warmth.
I had no great liking for the text. I was therefore not
open to criticism when I surrendered myself to the
delights of Bérard's décor and to my irrepressible
admiration for Jouvet, to whom all must be forgiven in
recognition of his inventiveness and tyrannical despotism.
Finally I had eyes only—I am coming to the point—for
Marguerite Moreno, totally absorbed in creating before
our eyes the part of La Folle. Such a store of apparent
naturalness, so perfectly simulated a disregard for the
audience, the control of a commanding voice in allotting
to each salient word in a clever sentence its due share
of sonority and rhythm, the audacious sallies of a dolled-
up warhorse, in short the orchestration of the rôle by an

incomparable artiste had in it the power to overwhelm us, and overwhelm us it did.

From the shadows of the stage-box I subjected Marguerite as indiscreetly as you please to the full force of my faculties, with an eye as critical as that of a dresser or stage manager.

I was soon reassured. Under the coating of black and white chalk, beneath the tinsel frippery of her clothes, a great artiste was observing us, a keen-eared musician was profiting by our silence just as much as by our applause. Once my fears were allayed, my pride assuaged, I was able that evening—it was, I think, the fifth performance —to forecast a long and triumphant run for Moreno, and prosperity for the Athénée.

That I might taste and enjoy to the full one dazzling pleasure only, I denied myself for once all interest in the writing, and I would not have exchanged my lack of warmth on that evening for no matter what brand of enthusiasm.

Moreno's inspiration in her part did not begin to wane till after several hundred performances. I have never much cared for the way the public have of judging a stage performance as they would a track event, and applying the term "exhausting" to the eighteen hundred lines or so that devolve upon La Folle. Passing serenely through both moments of anxiety and ovation, Moreno pursued her triumphant way once and often twice a day at the Athénée, yet still found time to visit me.

"But you don't even look tired!" I said in admiration.

"I am tired all the same," she said. "All those stairs to climb up and down! The dryness in the air that's so harmful to one's throat, the lengthy periods of standing about on the set . . ."

I interrupted her with a gesture she understood.

"Oh yes, I see, the exacting nature of my part! Macolette, bear in mind that if I don't look tired it's because I'm not very tired. What I have to do comes quite easily to me. La Folle is a very long part, an eccentric part requiring no great subtlety. It carries no mysterious psychological overtones, so it doesn't take a lot out of me. Would you like to know what I really think? No one has a better claim than you to be privy to it. It's my idea that anybody could play the part, no matter who. Only . . ."

She broke off to open her bag and go through the ritual of muttering: "My key—I've lost my key! Oh no, there it is! I've left my money on the mantelpiece. . . . And now what have I done with Pierre's letter!"

"Only," she resumed, "nobody realises it. On reflection, I think it would be best if nobody but us two ever did know it."

And now here I am giving it away, I, the faithless trustee of this strange confession that bears the stamp of excessive modesty and mystery-weaving fantasy, crying it aloud; but it no longer carries its confidential tone, its accompanying look. She left it with me one day just as she was making off under the wing of her felt hat— chestnut was it, or beige that day, or possibly aubergine!

I did not go a second time to hear *La Folle de Chaillot*. Moreno used to come occasionally to give me news of it, never failing to laugh at herself.

"Still going from strength to strength, Marguerite?"

"Still going strong. Between performances they bring along children for me to bless."

There would follow some anecdote or other that took her back, that took us both back into her past. Any resemblance she might have had to her mother—whose malevolent, well-preserved good looks I remember—assumed on her own lips the mordant quality of an inspired replica. When made up as an elderly woman in a comic film, she would suddenly remind me of her mother (as in *Les Jeux sont faits*) so forcibly, so majestically, as to be disconcerting. When she played the White Ghost in *La dernière Nuit de Don Juan*, one saw for the last time, between the folds of her tightly drawn veil, one saw the dazzle of beauty fall on features that for so long had disdained it.

I keep on looking all about me for Marguerite Moreno. While she was alive we could do without each other for long periods at a time. A telephone call or an exchange of letters would give me back across the space that separated us the tone of her voice and all its clarity. My colleagues, her friends and admirers have given me a bitter-sweet pleasure by printing in the papers an ever increasing number of likenesses hitherto unknown to me. I have been provided with all save her living presence.

Shortly before her death she had invited a grand-niece to stay with her. She had been incapable of hiding her astonishment, her deep feelings, at the sight of a human flower full of health and intelligence. This I deduce from her last letters, in which I find an affectionate constraint, a feeling of watchful pride, even to the extent of discovering something quite new to her, the freedom to welcome by name the idea of the future, at the suggestion

of a radiantly beautiful child. Yet in all this persisted a
reticence, blurred by a sort of timidity in speaking of the
future, of a state of permanency, in admitting the possibility of her life easing off as a result. Only after hesitation would she have sacrificed the poetic and wandering
use to which she had put the autumn of her days.
Her letters, which are the letters of an artist expert in
the choice of words, might cherish the idea of further
spiritual adventures, but surely, for her, the most en-
thralling project would have been to renounce the adven-
turous! A little prudence on her part, a less glacial March,
and Marguerite Moreno would still be with us. Or else,
some hundred miles from here, she might have preferred
to be free of the life-long fetters of her art in the enjoyment of her own wondrous blue spring, her vines and
cultivated lands, and enhanced family circle! "This
year," she wrote to me, "you are going to find a new
creature when you come to stay with me, so much has
everything changed since your first visit! This year you
are at last coming to live in my lovely countryside . . ."

At this point, I don't doubt, she paused in her writing
to let her eyes linger on her estate, on the jewelled blues
that the darting black-backed fish set flashing in her
spring waters, to let her ears listen for the cry of a very
small child. Yet this time, too, she did not dare to write
"home" in place of "countryside".

XI

HYSSOP, my dear Sir, it must be hyssop, this already shrivelled twig that still keeps its clinging scent and is almost as delicate as snow crystals. But I do not guarantee this. Just because Mermod's, the Swiss publishing firm, have issued a little book of mine, in which I speak of a few plants in the most familiar terms either informatively or to their detriment, it hardly deserves to be compared by you to *La Botanique des Dames*, an excellent work where you will see pictures of elegant ladies of the manor hunting for mushrooms in patent leather dancing-shoes and full flying flounces, and butterflies dying in agony under white-gloved fingers!

Yes, I incline to the view that it is hyssop. Starting from pure camphor, its scent runs the whole gamut of two or three chaste perfumes suggestive of capsicum, such as lavender and rosemary, before it ends up as—why, in heaven's name!—as hyssop. *Hysopo et mundabor!* Would you like me to sing to you over the telephone a good part of the mass in latin? I could. You would never believe your ears, my dear Sir with the good sense not to give your name, so you must take my word for it, that the little sweet-smelling herb is hyssop: myself, I take it for one of those presents that fly out from a letter, roll out of a

133

cabbage leaf or pill-box, in other words, one at which I should never dream of turning up my nose.

Before yours came today I had already received, from H. E. Brahim el Glaoui, a bottle from Marrakesh filled with some grey antimony, spangled and delicate, which goes by the name of kohl, koheul, or mokoheul—I cannot be sure which is the right name for it. What does the spelling matter, now that I am well supplied with cosmetic which can act as a surgical dressing, which prevents the eyes from reddening, allows one to face up to a strong light, sun or electric, and dust-laden air into the bargain : in short, the antimony they use throughout the orient to slip in between the eyelids of newborn babes!

For a great many years I religiously went to buy my koheul at Bichara's, "Syrian Perfumer", from a thin, slight, swart man whose handshake was always so dry and so gentle. He supplied all the very latest novelties, from clay for washing the hair to cakes of soap the shape of small cylinders that looked good enough to eat. I recollect that he never failed to touch wood when asking after my baby daughter, to protect her from the powers of evil. He spoke very low, in a tired voice, and coughed a discreet cough, which was to land him, discreetly enough, in the grave! A man with an aura of physical distinction about him, which gave his place of business an air of enchanted alchemy. He left a daughter who wrote poetry.

I am indebted to a lady from Oran, the wife of General C.—she had married a man of my father's year in the army, a young and dashing captain—for my daily habit of using antimony. A converted Jewess, the general's lady instructed me in many a nicety practised by inmates of the harem, among them the regular use of kohl. In her widowhood, she still affected some peculiarly African forms of adornment, such as hair-curlers of leather, ropes of blue pearls or necklaces of gazelle-droppings, and other magical fetishes, despite all of which she never missed going to mass on a Sunday. In Paris, where I once stayed with her for three weeks, I soon developed a liking for couscous and the plump sweetmeats of Oran.

All the same, I never dared to ask Sido, my mother, for leave to pay a second visit to Paris, or to tell her how one morning there I had happened upon the general's wife while she was busy supervising the household chores of a former batman turned house-boy. Perched high on a double ladder and wearing a blue apron, the lad was engaged in wiping the panes of a fan-light, to the accompaniment of a stream of advice from his Oranese mistress positioned at the foot of the ladder. " You short-arsed little runt," she cursed him roundly, " I can see from here the streaks and blurs you've left on the glass! What you want is a touch of encouragement, eh! " And with that she wantonly seized hold of him by the rump in so tight a grip that he whinnied with surprise and delight. Then he leapt down off the ladder and returned the compliment.

I was then at that uncompromising age when one denies to persons of advanced years the right to indulge in amorous love, when one takes exception to the slightest gesture which may give rise to love and disapproves most thoroughly should it find expression in unseemly high jinks. Far more than the playful prank played by Madame la Générale, it was the man's answering cackle that sent me indignantly back to the room I had just left. I was fifteen! The very age when one quivers with scandalised horror at the salacious behaviour of one's elders. At fifteen, love is on the brink of tears for a yes, for a no: it sees nothing to be amused at in the pinching of buttocks.

Like most dogs with big rounded heads—bull-dogs, bull-terriers, little Brabançon terriers, and boxers—her memory was acute. My elder brother's boxer bitch *knew* several songs, and Souci, my own French bull-dog bitch, an exceptionally large number of words: she was so quick in picking them up that for my own amusement I would give her a few faulty pronunciations. She adored fruit, with a marked preference for ripe raspberries and grapes, and to these, but solely for her own benefit, I gave the names of "raspbeeries" and "gripes". Sometimes, when this ritual had slipped my memory, I would say to her "Would you like a raspberry, or a grape?", and she would then give me a puzzled look and say nothing. I would then correct myself: "A nice little raspbeery? A gripe?", upon which Souci took heart at once and bounced forward full of overjoyed acquiescence. So it was until the day when she made the discovery that not only the vines but the raspberry canes as well bore their fruit within the reach of a full grown bull-dog; thereafter she dispensed with my help and my mispronounced vowels, and went out at seven in the morning to breakfast off raspbeeries and gripes.

I had bought her at the Tuileries Dog Show, where she had won First Prize for French bull-dogs, Class "7 kilos and under", and I had paid nine thousand francs for her. Her brother, sold for his weight in gold, went off to

America. This transaction made such a hole in my pocket that I had to forego my new tailor-made costume and afternoon " ensemble " in order to enrich Souci's wardrobe with a scarlet morocco-leather harness. It is possible that when we went out together the threadbare state of my right elbow and my felt hat (the one the Comtesse de Noailles called my " old huntsman's cap ") between them gave me a rather moth-eaten look, but the bitch attracted every eye. In all our eleven years together, Souci and I never encountered a similar couple where so much envious admiration was bestowed on the bull-dog.

For some little time before Souci's day, three of us were to be seen taking our constitutional in the Bois de Boulogne : Belle Aude, a sheep dog from the Beauce, on her high black-and-flame-coloured paws, myself on my bicycle, and Pati, the miniature terrier from Brabant, tucked away in a strawberry basket tied on to my handlebars. On reaching the less frequented rides, I would put the impetuous little lady from Brabant down on the ground, where she invariably did her best to outpace the huge shepherdess from the Beauce. Both came to heel only when the weight and effect of my words of command were fully appreciated because given in the vernacular.

More than one passer-by would remain stationary with surprise for a good minute, on observing that the two bitches were able to distinguish between their right and their left without the slightest hesitation, and of taking up their position on the nearside of my machine.

The Last Cat knew the melody of one song only, a pleasing American number, delightfully sung by the Sophomores, or by the Revellers. Sometimes, when she was sleeping the venerable sleep of cats I would put on the familiar record. She did not always completely wake up, but as she lay dozing a smile of dreamy connivance would blossom on her enchanting lips: "Yes, yes, I hear it. Don't wake me up altogether." I think the title of her song was "Blue Heaven". You may be sure that if and when I buy another gramophone, I intend to buy that record as well.

If ever I cease to sing the praises of the Last Cat, it will be when I no longer have anything to say about anything. Perhaps that day is not far off; but since it has not yet arrived, and since I have been able to tell only of what I know, I still have a word or two to say on this subject and on that, to prevent myself from falling back on my old loves: not that these bring a blush to my cheeks, or that I have any wish to run them down, but simply because there are more than enough of them. I have no longer any desire to look at myself in the mirror of the past with my hair in the style of a gentleman about town or, for that matter, adorned with a wreath of pompom roses.

The vogue for the chestnut poodle is clearly nearing its end, and that of the black cocker spaniel will not long survive it. Since the war, various breeds of sporting dog have acquired favour and high prices, principally the spaniel, mahogany red, or spotted black and white, or liver and white. You may come across them on the sidewalk, always on a lead, with that look of rational despair that befits a sporting dog up on a visit to Paris. They are certainly sagacious, as they wait, eyes down, in the banana-queue at the fruiterer's. Sagacious they may be, yet they are gifted with a singular aptitude for getting lost. "*Lost, between Rue de Miromesnil and the Gare de l'Est, setter with collar but no address . . . Lost, Breton*

*spaniel answering to the name of Gamin . . . Lost,
spaniel . . ."* Who is to blame? On whom should my
suspicion fall? Alas, poor spaniel! Like Madame de
Sévigné, you find that to you the Paris pavement is a
place of torment, where the pads of your paws dry up
and crack, accustomed as they are to roam the marshlands
and hidden ditches where the veronica speedwell grows!
"Take the dog with you, you'll exercise him in the
course of your shopping!" And then all of a sudden there
is no dog, no lead, only the net-bag full of lettuces,
Toulouse sausages, and never quite ripe enough bananas,
that, and a poor lady deprived of her spaniel. *"Lost,
Market Lane Albert-Ier . . . Lost, Saint-Honoré Market
. . ."* Perhaps to the sensitive, chamois-leather nostrils
of the spaniel there came, somewhere between the stall of
rotting oranges and the gypseous cheese stall, a whiff of
Rambouillet from the water-cress crate, of spring water,
the scent of a young rabbit or a bird, the smell that puts
wings on a spaniel's paws and brings madness to his
highly trained narrow mind. *"Lost . . . Large reward
offered . . ."*

Spurned by fashion, what will now become of the pro-
lific cocker, with his eight-pup litters, black as Erebus?
His masters may love him, as often as not, for his own
sake, for his incurable sentimentality. His two main
worries are an atavistic nostalgia for the chase and any
chance remark he has half overheard, to which ever after
he attaches an unkind intention. He dwells on these con-
tinually and sheds secret tears. We do our best to console
him for the sake of his beautiful sad eyes. "Come here,
my precious darling, and let me pin back your lovely long
ears so that they won't get soaked in your food!" At least

he will never join the ranks of the forgotten schnautzer with his gendarme's mustachios, or the bedlington with his frizzy lamb's wool, who always reminds me, because of the bump on his nose, of the late Duchess Sforza, *née* Antokolski! But that is impertinence enough with regard to the high and mighty persistent breeds, and Madame Steinbock-Fermor will tell you better than I what points to look for in a sleek bedlington.

The market for chestnut poodles is getting easier. Trading in jet-black poodles shows signs of recovery. The run on snow-white poodles is at a standstill. Little demand for curly-haired poodles. It is worth noting that certain poodle-fanciers remain faithful to the chestnut, to wit Mlle Hilda Gélis-Didot and Francis Carco. M. Watermann still keeps to the jet-black breed. I purposely forgot that one. I omit any mention of those clipped like topiary, their sensitive bare backs exposed to the nip of rheumatics and their bearded heads resembling Victor Hugo, or Bébé Bérard.

The vogue for the boxer is at its height. No canine character better deserves it, the bull-dog excepted. The female has all the virtues, friendliness and mother-love, and is so courageous in a fight that one fears for her life. I speak from personal experience of one called Gertrude, given us as a companion, short in the leg, fat as a sausage because overfed, whose bright eyes spangled with grains of gold dust earned her the nickname of "The lass with the golden eyes". She knew how to hate as well as to love, and would bare her teeth behind a curled back black lip to rivals of every race. But to each member of our family, hers by adoption, she meted out an impartial affection amounting almost to an intoxicated vocal display, for boxers sing and do everything but speak, and in this the cats were not excluded. O all you female boxers in your black masks creased with silky wrinkles! Here's a toast in your honour, and I don't mind saying that I am ready even now to be overcome with emotion when you go past me, leaving a trace of your short-haired racial odour, of warm ponies and clean-smelling breath! Your unforgettable way, entering body and soul into the family circle, there to sit and dream as you gaze at the fire, listening to the sound of voices, to thoughts, the last bang of the door closing, the overhead step on the ceiling!

Here, I think, is an *amende honorable* paid to the dog world. I have never boggled over them, but long experience has taught me that we are far too prone to excite the lyrical expression of a communicative dog. Three words in the special doggy tone of voice, a single pat, and a dog, quite unable to control his nerves, will break into his own language. "Get along with you," my mother would scold, "it will soon lead to tears." Handsome she was all the same, a sphinx with precious few secrets, as she sat there among us.

Her name was Gertrude. She used to sit on her creased haunches, like a naked woman, and dream as she stared into the fire. The life of an excitable dog is passing short.

That child, now, crying down there in the Garden, his mouth squarely open . . . He's been crying for some time. He puts me in mind of a Belgian child, who regularly started to cry at meal-times. Four to five years old, with lanky silken locks the colour of butter. In his relations with his weak-minded mother he always made use of the persistence which is the heritage of certain children, persistence on a scale to bring to the parent's face a sort of hunted look in which may be read the fleeting desire to see the death—to bring it about even!—of the child who is crying so shrilly. On one occasion this Belgian child, whose name was Jules, started to cry on sitting down at table and never left off. His soft-hearted mother did not send him packing, did not shut him up in the cellar or in the broom-cupboard.

He continued to bellow, with long-drawn, full-throated yells, while his mother, white as a sheet, said the first thing that came into her head. "Come, come, my pet . . . Jules, be quiet! A big boy like you, getting on for five! You won't get any whipped cream! If you don't shut up at once, Sir, you'll not go to mass—no, I mean the circus. My God, how miserable you make me feel! Why couldn't I have had a child who was dumb! Jules, I beg of you . . . Jules! obey your mother!"

Suddenly the child stopped short in the very midst of a bellow, whereupon the mother's face took on renewed colour and hope. She proceeded to give him crême Chantilly, gâteau de Savoie, dried plums, all of which he gobbled up. Next she treated him like a mother's little darling "was he feeling unhappy then!", and wiped his eyes and mouth. At once Jules started bellowing again, louder and more incurably than ever. His mother stared at him, trembling before the mystery. "But why," she ventured to ask, "why are you crying again?"

He dried up for long enough to answer with composure, "I had not finished crying."

I have never understood it, never tolerated, never made vain use of this outpouring, this crying scandal, this square-mouthed grimace as in the act of being sick. With a sort of horror I view the quaking chin, the convulsive twitch at the corners of the lips, all the apparent signs of a cold in the head magnified twenty thousand times, the blackmail which is all that an access of sobbing amounts to. At the root of this horror of mine is the indignation shown by Sido at the wanton tears of children. Later in my life, I came across a feeling similar to my own in the ugly, providential old English paragon who looked after my daughter for seven years, and who used to say to her when only two and a half "Cry! Are you not ashamed to cry in front of me and in front of your mama? You should no more cry in front of anyone than do your business with the door open!"

In our intimate talks together Miss Draper would make profession of her faith. "Crying is a bad habit, that and no more. My baby doesn't cry when she falls down or has to go up to bed." The catalogue of her infant charge's virtues was interrupted only for the purpose of outlining for the same child a whole series of well deserved punishments. In times of juvenile rebellion and crisis, it was a never-failing satisfaction to me to mark on my daughter's rosy-cheeked face the battle waged with tears, the lip bitten in proud restraint, the struggle, begun so early, for self-control.

Once upon a time, however . . . On one special occasion I had to take my daughter up from La Corrèze to Paris and Miss Draper could hardly be said to have entrusted her to me with good grace. Bel-Gazou was five at the time, and with her fresh complexion and boy's knickers she enjoyed in Paris the success that was her due. For three full weeks, between the circus and the cinema, she never gave the least sign that to be parted from her Nursie-dear was an infliction. It is true that I saw her fetch one or two yawns and occasionally pull a long face, but I put all this down to her Paris diet. Also the suspicion that it might have something to do with the frivolous habits of her paternal grandmother, who wanted to teach Bel-Gazou the tango along with some other social amusements.

We set off on the return journey, the child and I, back to the Limousin fields speckled with cows, and small country houses perched on the tip-top of the little hills. On the train I introduced some subject of conversation which my daughter sifted for the purpose of acceptance or rejection in her usual calm if rather distant manner. As we approached Varetz I pointed out to her, in the setting of the landscape she knew so well, all the wonders she seemed to have forgotten, the osier-beds, the farm-steads, the winding Vézère, haunt of kingfishers. We had no carriage to meet us at the station, but the little toy-train would be putting us down not far from home. I looked out of the window before we drew up and caught sight on the platform of the tall, military figure of Miss Draper.

"Darling! Bel-Gazou! Look, there's 'Miss' waiting for us on the station! Now mind you say how d'you do to her nicely."

There was no question of her saying how d'you do nicely! I had beside me a small creature who had just burst into a flood of tears that were rolling down her velvet cheeks without wetting them. So shaken with emotion was she that she never dreamed of getting down from the train and could only sob " Nursie-dear, ooh-ooh-ooh! Nursie-dear! Nursie! "

There and then I learnt that a very small child can weep for joy in just the same way as a lovesick maid. As for Miss Draper! Never have I seen a gendarme at a country station weep so unashamedly, in full view of his half-section.

Before a moment was out, as we were crossing over the line, my daughter and her nurse were back in their usual state of estimable dissembling. My daughter was painting a vivid description of Paris, with an air of complete disdain for Le Long-Pré nestling among its flowers below her. Stiffly Nursie-dear was thrusting behind her all the seductive pleasures she had never experienced: " If you love Paris so much, you would do better to stay there. For my part, I've found it most peaceful here without you to plague the life out of me! "

The child down there in the Garden is still crying, but intermittently, now that his mother is gone. The enclosure being relatively free from dangers, children can be left there by themselves to learn about life, early and on their own, according to the codes of language and activity established during the last war. The crying ceases each time that the turning-out of a mud-pie (in the proportions of 50 per cent moist earth to 50 per cent droppings of various denominations) makes a call on the child's fingers. After that he starts whimpering again, but without real conviction. Another small boy now comes out from the shelter of the arcades, advances right up to the wire-netting round the lawn, lifts his head and shouts, as though summoning the pigeons, "Nah then, yer two muckers! 'Ave I ter come and take you by the . . ."

His shouts at once arouse a pretty little fair-haired girl, and a big curly-haired boy, who still stumbles as he walks. The trio move off. They are old acquaintances of mine, about whom I know almost all there is to be known, as you are now about to hear. Jojo, the eldest, is seven; he has reached the stage of his first year at school. A Paris street-urchin like so many others. Distinguishing marks: none. For cheek is not a distinguishing mark.

His sister, la Carrée, is four and a half. She is a pretty child, well filled-out, always with a cold hanging about her.

Their mother is a tired woman. Distinguishing marks: none. Tiredness is not a distinguishing mark in mothers with three children.

The Last, a boy of twenty-nine months.

Jojo, on coming home from school, hurls off his satchel with the authentic heave of the shoulders of an old salt.

"I've made it. I'm taken on."

His Mother: "Taken on? Taken on where?"

"Choir-boy. At Saint-Eustache."

"Since when?"

"I start—Sunday."

"You a choir-boy! I never heard such a thing! You're joking!"

"Joking! I'll say I'm joking! There's money in it—d'you get that! It pays. The pal who put me on to the fiddle has five hundred francs in his money-box already. Talk of a job! You fiddle a bit here, you fiddle a bit there. You say the mass. You fiddle a bit on that. I'm on to something, I tell you!"

"All the same, Jojo, you're not telling me that sort of thing can be fixed without the parents' consent! You're still under age—you can't go making your own agreements with curés! Even supposing your father . . . (*There follow many superfluous words that seem to have nothing to do with either Jojo, la Carrée, or the Last.*)

The following Sunday Jojo has a long lie abed, waiting his turn at the foot-bath.

His Mother (*with, for once, superior irony*): "Well, I thought you were going to mass?"

Jojo: "I've chucked it."

"Because why?"

"Because of the time, first. It's too early. And because of the métro. With the price they charge you for fares, I'd be lucky not to be out of pocket. I've given it a miss."

"And how about your tooth?"

"Still in. It moves a bit but it's still in. Look!"

"It's gone on for long enough. Tomorrow I'm taking you to the dentist."

"And what'll that cost you?"

"About two hundred, I don't doubt."

"Bit steep! (*Thinks*) M'man, will you pay me over the two hundred if I bring you the tooth tomorrow?"

"First bring me the tooth, then we'll see."

Jojo (*in the afternoon*). "There you are! (*He puts the small incisor into his mother's hand and then holds out his own.*) My two hundred?"

"Your two hundred! Two hundred francs to a child of your age? Two hundred francs, when a person such as me finds it hard enough to earn as much? I never heard such a thing!" (*Jojo howls. Interchange of loud cries.*

Jojo gets fifty francs. Appeasement. Momentary childish-
ness.)

    Jojo (in good humour): "Hi, la Carrée! What d'you
say to a game of marbles? "

    Voice of la Carrée: "No! It's raining in the garden."

    Jojo: "We'll play on the landing. We'll make the pot
in the hole left by the missing tile."

    (*Silence. Enter la Carrée with blood on her mouth. She
is crying, but making no fuss about it.*)

    Jojo (interested): "What ever's the matter with you? "

    La Carrée: "The bit of string cut me. I wanted to pull
out a tooth with a bit of string."

    Jojo: "Never knew you had one loose. Which tooth
is it? "

    La Carrée: "No, it's not loose. I wanted to touch fifty
francs."

    (*Explosion of cries in the next room. Maternal cries,
and cries from the Last.*)

    His Mother: "Now what's up with him? What's
wrong with him? What a curse it is to have a child like
that! Just take a look at him! His mouth all cut to pieces!
To go and slash himself like that when he's only twenty-
nine months old! What are children coming to these
days, I ask you! "

    La Carrée (aside to Jojo): "Don't let on. He's been
trying to get a tooth out with the tin-opener. He wanted
to touch fifty francs! "

Since December we have gone back to being ten at the
Académie Goncourt. Lucien Descaves, however, a brisk
octogenarian, is kept at home by his great age, a friend

become fragile now and light as a vine-shoot. I have always enjoyed the Goncourt Lunches, even in the days of abstentions, frictions, and cleavages, when no more than five or six places would be laid. If there were not that little lift at Drouant's, I should certainly be rather cut off from my enjoyment; but then I could rely on the clasped hands of three or four men prepared to haul me up to the salon adorned by the flaky portrait of Edmond de Goncourt, and there I would settle down content. For we are a mixed company, fervent in our agreement to differ and wholly rebellious to the idea of unanimity. Dorgelès never misses an opportunity of going pop like a chestnut roasting on a brazier. Carco gets a fit of the sulks every now and again, when he relapses into silence and deprives us of the delightful timbre of his voice, that of a trained singer (the finest voice of any on the radio!). Larguier has the mischievous humour, and mane, of a playful lion, and roars in alexandrines. As for Billy? Billy knows everything that I do not know: that surely must make him the fountain-head of knowledge!

It is no good my posing as an old buck, for I still thoroughly enjoy the intensely feminine pleasure of being the only woman at the Goncourt Lunches, where I sit surrounded by a veritable Areopagus of men—five, six eight, nine of them. And real men, worthy of the name— age does not enter into it—with all the faults and attrac- tions of the male sex. Descaves has to be seen to be believed when he bangs on the table the size of a wheat- field, which destroys all confidence and intimacy, or when he submits the wines to the test of his nostrils or his tongue, or criticises the cooking; Rosny-jeune too, highly qualified to be present was a good sight, ruddy-cheeked as an apple in autumn, his memory and hearing as sound as ever for all his eighty-seven years! I perceive, and derive comfort from the solicitude they do their best to conceal. They have the air, one and all, of remembering the woman I was once. From time to time our dashing last-elect, Gérard Bauer, inscribes a "paper" to me in words affectionate as a love-letter! I should like, as I glance at the round table, to put on record that Arnoux botanises like an angel gardener, and that Carco expounds on the radio his novel method of writing history. But at our meetings one person, and one person only, is sub-jected to our praise or dispraise, the candidate: we do battle solely on behalf of outsiders. And I behave like the others, as I sit among my male colleagues who bear the outward signs of hard work, and often enough of weari-ness and ripe old age, and who, good men and true that they are, lose their tempers, raise their voices, blaspheme. Like any other human beings, they quarrel among them-selves, but, thank heavens, they enjoy their food! Not one among them has lost his zest for writing or his admiration for authors. What else is there, other than this love and devotion, to sustain us, year by year, along the hard high road of the literature we have to read? For read we do. We read a hundred to a hundred and twenty books. We read novels of four hundred up to eight hundred pages long. Once the time has come, we demolish, we scatter to the four winds, the solid brick wall that has lined my room. "Fortunately," say some of my friends in a flippant and knowing tone of voice, "you don't need to know their full contents, you can pick and choose at will." No, that we cannot, even supposing we were so minded. I tell you once again, we read. A strange assembly indeed, that out of ten members numbers ten conscientious readers! Scrupulous, fallible, capable of making allowances for the still immature writer, of doing justice to youthful promise and living to regret it the following year! Does anyone imagine us to be reclining on a bed of roses when the bell rings for the last hour of the competitions? Our perplexities are summed up in a few faintly humorous lines for the evening papers: "With the help of the traditional oysters and the renowned *Blanc de Blanc*, all ten members of the Académie. Goncourt are to be found gathered together at this time . . ." But no, no, things were not as gay as that when the time for the white wine and the casting of votes came along. Unanimous on Salacrou, but I could have wished for Anouilh too. Cheers for Hériat, but Miomandre has been too long forgotten. And then, why not Robert Kemp?

For me to feel happy, the Ten would have to be increased to twenty—at least.

This evening my room has the appearance of a robbers' cave: it is one of the days on which a jeweller neighbour of mine amuses himself, and amuses me still more, in pouring out over my table the contents of the velvet-lined case in which he carries round his latest treasures. Before my eyes is a gold clip, studded with sapphires. I can see a snail-shell embossed with turquoises in which has been reset a vivid though half-concealed little watch hardly bigger than a freckle. A heavy bracelet, most delicately wrought for its weight, has contrived to slip out to go and have a drink at my half-filled tumbler, as might a tame grass-snake. It is watched by the green eye of a chrysolite, a massive chrysolite ringed with brilliants, all that could be wished for to load a slender little finger and put the finishing touch to the mauve varnish of a convex nail.

Unguarded, an aquamarine pendant strays under my magic blue to replenish its own blue waters but these have been impounded with the thinnest network of tiny diamonds and enchained with gold. Thus it will have to wait, pendent, till it finds the more favourable shadows of the cleft between two breasts. Now where on earth has that heart-shaped tourmaline disappeared to? A moment since it was playing about with its all but wine-coloured pinks and reds between two turquoises. "Perhaps in the waste-paper-basket," my jeweller neighbour suggests, being a man of dry humour. The walls of my room are splashed with the dazzling glories of a Persian fairy tale as they catch the flashing sparkles from the unfathomable facets of the cut stones. That opaque contribution to the feast of colour—the turquoises—does something to assuage my own particular disorder. My friend and neighbour, the jeweller, assures me that the contemplation of precious stones brings relief to arthritic pains, that the majority of the gems snatched from the bowels of the earth are of beneficent effect. "Beneficent! What about the opal?" —"The opal too."—"But think of its reputation! Think of the well-attested instances when it has brought bad luck!" My neighbour shrugs his shoulders. "There have always existed clumsy folk who can't hammer in a nail without crushing their finger. They will always be with us. Take a particular look at this setting for a ring. I rather think it is my own invention. 'Knitted gold', it is called. Do you like it?"

Its mesh is certainly fine enough to merit the name
"knitted"—or "netted", as we used to say in my part
of the country—each link atwinkle so that it appears
sprinkled with a fine sand of diamonds: definitely, I like
"knitted gold". What else is there that I like? This fat
chalcedony tortoise, smoky and star-spangled as the night
sky over Paris? No, I don't much care for it. It reminds
me of an idiotic craze for inlaying the shells of baby
tortoises while still alive. That dainty flowering spray of
beryls? I don't care for that either. It is too showy for
my taste. Let me have, rather, that bracelet of knotted
pliant cord, distinctive, oriental, a symbol of wealth and
respectability. I praise it unreservedly, I try it on. And
since, the Lord be praised, I can admire without coveting,
possess all without acquiring, I savour a pleasure which
itself is many-faceted, one which stems from a thoroughly
Parisian art, the fruit of inventiveness and patience,
requiring manual dexterity in a high degree . . . When
I dub my neighbour artisan, he blushes with the pride
of a man rewarded.

By improving my acquaintance with him, I am able
to increase my familiarity with an expansive taste in which
I have never indulged. I learn any number of names. I
finger the lovely yellow metal, cold at first but quickly
warming to the touch, the abettor of so many crimes and
wars. More than once, anticipating its eventual recipient,
have I held in my hands some gorgeous plaything long
promised and awaited with feverish impatience. In the
hollow of my hand I have held a precious stone, naked as
a slave without a master. I might well have believed it to
be a live ember I was smothering, so curiously did its
darting red and yellow fires glow within it. But my

neighbour shrugged his shoulders. "Pfui . . . that's a mere nothing. Even its name, a fanciful one at that, is of little account. There is not a single orange-coloured stone that is of value. If ever we break away from rubies, emeralds, and sapphires, or struggle to free ourselves from diamonds, we come back for all that to the diamond, the emerald, and the ruby. Or else we have to fall back on these other stones! "

These other stones I find charming, with names suggestive of liquid and transparent essences: the peridot, in which the bronze green always shows true, the vari-coloured tourmaline, the easily accessible ruby spinel, the blue-green aquamarine, ever true to its name; and there is little danger of my forgetting you, my facetious chrysoberyl, green in the morning and turning red at night, such are the pleasing dissonances wrought in you by my blue lantern!

"Well, in that case, why do you not fall back on these other stones? "

But the master of the velvet-lined case showed little else but resignation as far as they were concerned.

"Pretty enough in their way," said he. "Amusing. I quite like using them as paving stones on cigarette-cases, as plaques on belts, as anything on a large scale. Up till now they have mistakenly been put to finicking uses. It would take more than our entire stock of ingenuity to give them what they lack . . ."

"And what may that be? My dear friend, you are on the verge of falling victim to the kind of snobbery that consists in reproaching them for their lack of hardness, popularity, rarity, consistency . . ."

He put a stop to my words by raising his hand, before he delivered a disconcerting monosyllable. "No," he said. "The real truth is that they lack the genuine look."

My evening visitors never fail me. Yesterday it was the small grey and green parrot with Maria Lydis. Last week I had that nice little woman, Madame Margat, and her female chameleon. Yes, my dear Miomandre, a female chameleon, just think of it! I doubt her long surviving her tiny mate, killed by our climate. She used to sleep in his arms, and he hugged her tight all the night long. Once bereft of her husband, she no longer wanted to go on living. After a few days she consented to eat a little, but her lustreless skin hung loose. The nice lady who brought her along to me set down her cage on my bench-table, beneath the blue lantern, and slowly, slowly, as if drawn by a magnet, the chameleon started to climb towards the source of light and heat. Once she had reached the roof of the cage, she again became quite motionless. We are always adepts at placing the right barrier, be it roof or wall, between an animal and liberty. Clinging tight by hands and tail to some leafy branches, the chameleon gradually assumed over the surface of her skin the varied harmony of their greens; meanwhile she kept flashing one or other of her eyes towards the lamp, so that they resembled a Directoire lorgnette in miniature.

I watch, I ask questions. I know so little about chameleons. But I had the presence of mind to refer Mme Margat to Francis de Miomandre, and that was something to the good. It was also good to learn from

Mme Margat that the small, lovely creature sometimes climbs to the top of a bottle and there reclines her chin on the cork. That in the evening she returns to her solitary abode among the leaves. That she sometimes instals herself in the fruit basket and puts her arm round a banana. That she licks the moist inside of a pear-peeling.

I do not always possess the courage and good sense to turn away from my door those whom I call my " evening visitors ", be they birds, cats or dogs. They leave a wake behind them, the mark of creatures with whom I have exchanged credentials. I delight in nothing but their presence, and their departure drives me on to a growing sense of destitution, to a decision to forego the touch and sight of them, the coat, the paw, the deep-set eyes, the smile. My evening visitors normally make my time their own: they keep burning within me the persistent element of a flame, and of a dialogue. The Carcos' poodle (chestnut) deigns to endure boredom here from time to time. The poodle (chestnut) of Hilda Gélis-Didot is next in turn, but derives the same cold comfort. His name is Unic: he vents his impatience in huge sighs, looks at the time, deposits at the feet of his mistress a glove, a leash, a bag—all of them objects of a highly suggestive character. If Hilda pays no attention to them, Unic gives up, makes a melancholy meal off a detective story, or a sandal, or the small hearth brush. What a change is here from the worldly cheer of a parrot! Anatole-of-the-entresol sings, mimics to the best of his ability the bark of a watch-dog, the mewing of a cat, the human voice. And I would advise any burglar to keep away from his curved beak which can cut clean through a cutlet bone.

Yesterday evening the other parrot, the one belonging

to Mariette Lydis, took a strong dislike to his transport waggon when he had to reinstate himself in it. The bird is hardly bigger than a quail and dumb except for a very low cry. Back in his prison again, he took to demanding his immediate release by striking, time after time, three hard blows with his beak against the wooden side in perfect ryhthm: tock-tock-tock . . . tock-tock-tock. There is not a country in the world where prisoners and captives do not talk to each other in the language of tapping. But where had he learnt to count up to three, and even to three times three times three?

In this way there has been built up between animals and myself an understanding which has at times enriched and at others darkened my life. Each of my friends contributes something to it. From America I am sent cuttings from the illustrated papers in which I see that a bluish-grey cat is the model for baby linen de luxe and hats made to her size, that a dozen branches of the New York subway have been immobilised one after the other to allow the rescue of a fine tom-cat that had fallen into the cavity of a ventilation-shaft, that another tom-cat is able to open various locks and latches by a series of combined movements. But "Mimile" Blanchar is just as cunning without her picture ever having appeared in the papers. News from Bordeaux: a fine boxer bitch has just presented to the world a litter of eleven pups! (Madame Colette, what are we to do? They are all quite enchanting, but my bitch will soon be worn out. What advice can you give me?" Answered: "Buy good-milker-nanny-goat.")

News from elsewhere: "Madame Colette, I have at your disposal a pretty little sea-horse." I remember the proposals of Père Raux: "Wouldn't you care for a lovely lion-cub of four months? She sleeps on my bed." No, I do not want a pretty little sea-horse. Not even a tender octopus with great dreamy eyes, like the one that used to snuggle down caressingly into the hollowed hands of its keeper and friend at the Oceanographical Museum in Monaco. Above all, not an ape unjustly punished for its sins by looking like a sad little man!

A lonely little female chameleon; a Polish nightingale; a couple of parrots; a gentle, jovial boxer, Zorro Piguet, the colour of pig-skin, heavy as a tight-packed valise; the tiny pekingese, whose short life was entirely given over to the passionate worship of Germaine Fraysse; Crockie de Polignac, the golden basset-hound subject to nervous pregnancies—it is a short list, the list of my evening visitors. The Eden permitted us has nothing of a Noah's Ark about it.

The only living animal left to me that I can call my own is the fire. It is my guest, and the work of my hands. I know all about covering a fire, succouring a fire. I know the art of surrounding a fire in the open air with a circular trench, so that it may burn up well without "marking" the stubble and setting the ricks ablaze. I am well aware of its dislike of even numbers, that three logs burn better than two and seven than four, and that like every other animal it likes having its belly scratched from underneath.

Between it and me lies an old question which it takes me most of my time to resolve since it burns on my hearth for three-quarters of the year, there in my bedroom which has adopted its colours, red and white, and its presence. I burn it ceaselessly. Ceaselessly, but with a certain thriftiness. I pile it up, but with the air of doling out beggarly alms. I show it that I am a native of a distant province, where everyone learns not to waste wood and bread. I give it its quota of splinters, twigs and dried leaves, and I intend always to have the last word with it— that stand-by of trainers acquired through long dealings with animals. It repays me, by hurling itself upon the least of my offerings; it makes much of me, encourages me in my by now automatic incantations to it: the business of incantation loses nothing by it.

The hearth at which I solemnise my fire worship is of ancient construction and required, I don't mind betting, no more than the hand of a simple mason to build it. Within the precincts of the Palais-Royal we do have here and there some door-furniture and wainscot-panelling of artistic merit, along with a few fine fire-places. The marble has been stripped away from my own and replaced by a sort of pink and beige galantine. No matter, it has kept its intrinsic nature and its appetite for heat, together with that allegiance of permanent fixtures devised to share intimately in the life of man and his rudimentary needs.

Anyone who is given to meditating in front of a fire, during the hours when the shades of night beyond the window panes guarantee him safe protection, need no longer fear being joined at the fireside by the dog and the wolf of twilight—the shudder and the sudden start. Only novices in the art are liable at that time to be assailed so powerfully by age, fright, evil, or a guilty conscience. Let me run through my little incantation.

A fire affords such genial company
To the chill prisoner, the drear night long!
Close by my side there sits a good fairy
Who drinks, or smokes, or sings an ancient song . . .

Whose lines are those? I might almost go so far as to say they are my own, since once upon a time a competition for reading aloud was held in my canton for those of us who, when twelve or thirteen, were made to read with meaning and expression from both verse and prose. A certain well-intentioned man, having heard in our chief town that no child in the district had any conception how to read other than in a monotonous drone, was roused to indignation and, after pointing out the dire peril into which the ignorance prevailing in the department of Yonne could not fail to plunge the whole of France, founded an elocution prize. A red and gold volume, and a diploma, confirmed that at the age of twelve-and-a-half Gabrielle-Sidonie Colette knew how to read, and consoled me for having slurred my words while reading, so that I said "who drink sore smokes", and inadvertently altered the prose of Madame de Sévigné.

A fire affords such genial company
To the chill prisoner . . .

Perhaps these second-rate verses really are mine. Mine as is the fire, as is everything that surrounds me at night.

Poetry does not necessarily have to be beautiful to stick in the depths of our memory, there to occupy most mischievously the place doomed to invasion by certain melodies which, however blameworthy, can never be expunged.

" A fire affords . . ."

Reading at night is a fickle ally. More reliable than a book is the setting I have arranged in honour of the

minutes and the hours. I am not always equal to my
bouts of insomnia, but I usually succeed in getting even
with them by the application of a sort of mental restora-
tive, which drives away fear of the unwonted from my
mind and my surroundings. It is not later than three
in the morning, nothing at roof-level is yet beginning
to pale. By reason of there being a lamp on every
pillar, I could count the number of arches along the
Palais-Royal from my bed. The inhabitants of this house
are so quiet that I never hear a soul at night; but the
clatter of my tongs into the grate would ruin the fitful
rest of even someone sleeping two doors away. Now, if
I am lying here motionless tonight, there is good reason
for it, for I can feel stirring within me—apart from
the twisting pain, as if under the heavy screw of a wine-
press—a far less constant turnscrew than pain, an insur-
rection of the spirit which in the course of my long life
I have often rejected, later outwitted, only to accept it in
the end, for writing leads only to writing. I am still going
to write; I say this in all humility. For me there is no
other destiny. But when does writing have an end? What
is the warning sign? A trembling of the hand? I used to
think that it was the same with the completed book as
with other finished ploys, you down tools and raise the
joyful cry "Finished!", then you clap your hands only
to find pouring from them grains of sand you believed
to be precious. That is the moment when, in the figures
inscribed by those grains of sand, you may read the
words "To be continued . . ."